Whetu Moana

Contemporary Polynesian Poems in English

EDITED BY Albert Wendt

Reina Whaitiri &

Robert Sullivan

UNIVERSITY OF HAWAI'I PRESS
HONOLULU

First published 2003

University of Hawai'i Press
2840 Kolowalu Street
Honolulu
Hawai'i 96822
http://www.uhpress.hawaii.edu

ISBN 0 8248 2756 2

Library of Congress Cataloguing-in-Publication Data
Whetu moana : contemporary Polynesian poems in English / selected and introduced by
Albert Wendt, Reina Whaitiri and Robert Sullivan.
p. cm.
Includes bibliographical references and index.
ISBN 0-8248-2756-2 (alk. paper)
1. Pacific Island poetry (English) 2. Islands of the Pacific—Poetry.
3. Pacific Area—Poetry. 4. Polynesia—Poetry I. Wendt, Albert, 1939- II. Whaitiri, Reina, 1943-
III. Sullivan, Robert, 1967-
PR9645.65.W48 2003
820.8'099965—dc21   2002045414

Cover design: Christine Hansen

Printed by Astra Print Ltd, Wellington, New Zealand

Whetu Moana

Contents

Introduction

Polynesia, the very word is polymorphic. It conjures up multiple images: warm tropical seas, palm-fringed lagoons, grass huts, semi-naked dusky maidens, portraits of Captains Cook and Bligh, even Kevin Costner and Elvis Presley. While the area known as Polynesia is indeed incredibly beautiful, it is also home to many thousands of people who have learned over the centuries to survive extraordinary hardships. The romantic ideas and images held by outsiders about the Pacific have plagued our people since first contact; and breaking away from the rest-and-recreation stereotypes has been a major issue for Polynesian writers, artists, scholars and politicians ever since.

Polynesia, Melanesia and Micronesia are the cultural regions of the Pacific. The Melanesians and Micronesians settled the Pacific starting about 50,000 years ago. Our Polynesian ancestors settled about 3000 or 4000 years ago, and they named the ocean, Te Moana Nui a Kiwa. The names for the three regions and the distinctions between them were established over the last 200 years, mostly by outsiders, sometimes by ourselves. The distinctions are not marked and outsiders may find it difficult to distinguish Tongan from Samoan or Niuean from Maori, for example, but we respect the differences between our cultures and take great pleasure in drawing attention to them.

When Polynesians first came into the region, they couldn't have known much about the Pacific's boundaries; they acquired that knowledge as they explored and settled the islands that stretched across the vast sea. The sky and the sea must have seemed both boundless and eternal to the early Polynesians, for how the people lived and connected with one another was determined by how well they understood and could control these two elements. This immense space of sea and sky was, and continues to be, the known world of the Polynesian. Our view of the world is unique, it is as broad and deep as it is high, and unlike those who come from continents or large bodies of land, we see a world with few limits. The people of Polynesia carefully and meticulously recorded their whakapapa, or lineage, thus establishing and strengthening their links with the earth, the sky, the gods and each other. Polynesians also believe that when we die we become the stars that help to guide the living across that huge body of water Te Moana Nui a Kiwa. The people learned how to read and work with their world, they learned about reading the ocean currents, the winds and stars, using that knowledge to sail and navigate their lives by. That is why we have called this anthology *Whetu Moana, Ocean of Stars*, which incorporates the concepts of sea, sky and stars. The title also suggests the variety of poets and poetry in the anthology, and their roots in Te Moana Nui a Kiwa and in their various cultures.

Polynesia extends from Hawaii (to the north-east) across to Rapanui (Easter Island) and down to Aotearoa/New Zealand in the south-west. Within that triangle are Tonga, Samoa, the Cook Islands, Niue, Tokelau, and the Society Islands. There are also Polynesian enclaves, like Rotuma, within Melanesia. These countries range from high volcanic islands to atolls, from snow-capped peaks to blue lagoons. This anthology is confined to poetry from most of the countries mentioned because they are English-speaking but, because of an accident of history, it is forced to exclude work from French-speaking Polynesia.

Over the last 200 years, under the influences of colonialism first from Europe, then America and Asia, our cultures have changed rapidly. Religion, diet, transport, housing, communication, every facet of life has been influenced by the colonial influx. As well, many of our people now include other ancestry, such as European and Asian, in their whakapapa. The peoples of the Pacific have always intermarried with other island groups, including Melanesia and Micronesia.

Since the 1950s decolonisation has taken place, and while most of our nations are again politically independent some, such as Aotearoa, Hawai'i and the Society Islands, remain colonised. Polynesian people within these countries are now minorities striving for their political independence and are intent on saving and developing their cultures. Literature and the arts are part of the decolonisation process and help define new cultures as they emerge from colonial influences as free and independent nations.

Polynesia was written into existence by outsiders and that literature has created many myths about our region. From about 1950 Polynesians have been writing back, presenting our view of the world and placing our people and places at the centre. All these changes are evident in the poetry we have selected, which reveals an interconnected web of linguistic, thematic, and worldviews. There is a commonality in our bubbling polyglot Polynesian diversity, the commonality of the ocean, of a shared vocabulary, of our communal cultures and values, and our colonial experience. These are the forces that draw our poetries together.

There are many western myths surrounding our region, ranging from Mead's fascination with the sexual, to the cardboard, plastic culture of the tourist trade and the myths surrounding Captain Cook. We hope this anthology succeeds in shifting the western gaze from current and historical myths onto the expressive reality of the poets included here.

Being Polynesians who love poetry, we wanted to look at the poetry that has developed in our region over the last two decades, and through that poetry to look at what has happened and is happening to ourselves and our cultures. Poetry is one of our most ancient art forms and is still respected and loved by our peoples. How are those ancient poetic traditions manifested in the new poetry? We wanted to create a collection that makes it possible to examine this.

But why have we focused only on poetry in English? There are over forty indigenous languages plus English, French, Portuguese, Spanish, Japanese and others in Polynesia. It is simply impossible to anthologise all those languages. English is more than 200 years old in our region, and is now one of the major languages of communication. English has become a Pacific language. In fact, it has become many Englishes in Polynesia, with each Polynesian country indigenising it for its own use. So now we have Maori English, Samoan English, Hawaiian English and so forth. Many pidgins have emerged too, such as Hawaiian Creole English. The languages of the colonisers have been, and continue to be, enriched and revitalised with the introduction of Polynesian words and concepts.

The content of this anthology reflects that rich diversity in English and pidgin. Many of our poets are bilingual but have chosen to write mainly in English; others are not fluent in their indigenous languages and so write only in English.

The task of collecting, reading and selecting the poetry from the breadth of Polynesia was quite daunting. By word of mouth and advertising we gathered the poetry of a range of established, mid-career, and exciting new poets.

We wanted to publish as many poets as we could and did not want the price of the anthology to be outside the reach of our communities so we decided to limit the anthology to about 300 pages. To do that, we decided not to include poems from two previous anthologies, *Lali* and *Nuanua*. The selection of poets in this anthology should be read as complementary to the previous volumes. We also decided to select work from only the last two or three collections by our established and much anthologised poets, so again, their selections should be read in tandem with the other anthologies.

We have arranged the poets by alphabetical order of surname in *Whetu Moana* rather than by countries, as in *Lali* and *Nuanua*. Our purpose is to juxtapose the poetries of the Pacific to generate views of

culture that are both common and strange, to see Polynesian poetry through a prism creating many coloured bands: age, language, place, polity and gender are some that leap out.

We have chosen poetry that we find exciting and interesting and that gives a representative view of Polynesia. We have limited the selection to poetry written by Polynesians since 1980. We didn't seek out particular themes, and selected from the poems that were available to us. The poems show a rich diversity, from poems of anger and protest by poets from countries where colonialism is alive and well, to those expressing respect and concern for the environment. But like poetry elsewhere many of the poems are about ordinary issues such as feelings, family, spirituality, ownership of land and our place in the world.

We anticipate that the poetry of Polynesia will continue to develop in new unexpected directions twenty years from now, just as our own history has developed. We sincerely hope that this anthology is a true reflection of Polynesian poetry today, that it will serve as a reference point for the future, and will be a useful teaching resource at all educational levels.

Over the long period of time taken to compile this anthology, many people have helped and advised us. We are particularly grateful to Elizabeth Caffin, Annie Irving, Katrina Duncan, and Christine O'Brien of Auckland University Press for their detailed and expert assistance, and their friendship and aroha/alofa.

Albert Wendt, Reina Whaitiri
and Robert Sullivan
September 2002

ACKNOWLEDGEMENTS

The editors and publisher are grateful to all the poets and copyrightholders for permission to reproduce the poems in this book. They were unfortunately unable to make contact with a small number of the poets but would be glad to hear from them at the earliest opportunity. They acknowledge the following publications in which some of the poems originally appeared: poems by Cherie Barford in *Plea to the Spanish Lady* (Hard Echo Press); by Alistair Campbell in *Stone Rain* (Hazard Press), *Gallipoli and other Poems* and *Maori Battalion* (both Wai-te-ata Press); by David Eggleton in *South Pacific Sunrise* and *People of the Land* (both Penguin); by Rangi Faith in *Unfinished Crossword* (Hazard Press); by Sia Figiel in *To a Young Artist in Contemplation* (Pacific Writing Forum); by Marewa Glover in *Hui* and *Mooncall*; by Rore Hapipi in *He Reo Hau* (Reeds), by Keri Hulme in *The Silences Between* and *strands* (both Auckland University Press); by Imaikalani Kalahele in *Kalahele* (Kalamakū Press) and *Prints and Poems*; by Māhealani Kamauu in *Ho'omanoa* (Kupuu'a Inc); by Kauraka Kauraka in *Dreams of the Rainbow*; by Phil Kawana in *Attack of the Skunk People* (Huia); by Vasa Leota in *Our Place in the Sun* (Pacific Islands Education Unit); by Trixie Menzies in *Papakainga*, *Rerenga* and *Uenuku* (all Waiata Koa); by Michael O'Leary in *Con Art* and *Nor Nothing I* (both Original Books); by Roma Potiki in *Stones in her Mouth* (IWA) and *Shaking the Tree* (Steele Roberts); by John Pule in *The Shark that Ate the Sun* and *Burn my Head in Heaven* (both Penguin) and *Bond of Time* (Pacific Writing Forum); by Caroline Sinavaiana-Gabbard in *Alchemies of Distance* (Tinfish Press and USP); by J. C. Sturm in *Dedications* and *Postscripts* (both Steele Roberts); by Robert Sullivan in *Piki Ake!* and *Star Waka* (both Auckland University Press); by Apirana Taylor in *Soft Leaf Falls of the Moon* (Pohutukawa Press); by Konai Helu Thaman in *Songs of Love* and *Kakala* (both Mana Publications); by Hone Tuwhare in *Shape-shifter* (Steele Roberts) and *Piggy-back Moon* (Godwit); by Albert Wendt in *Photographs* and *The Book of the Black Star* (both Auckland University Press); by Briar Wood in *Virago New Poets* and *Leave to Stay* (both Virago). Poems have also appeared in the following magazines and journals: *Bamboo Ridge*, *Climate*, *Kuleana*, *Mana*, *Manoa*, *Poetry New Zealand*, *Southern Ocean Review*, *Tinfish*.

VINEPA AIONO

Born in Western Samoa in 1960, Vinepa Aiono writes poems which deal with the personal pressures of growing up in the 1960s in Otara, South Auckland, and with the experiences she has gained in adulthood from working in that area as a social worker. She discovered poetry under the tutelage of an English teacher in the sixth form and has continued to write amateur poetry and perform her work only in the company of close friends. Vinepa currently works for Waitemata Health in the child abuse area.

Adapting

Uncle! Wear a jersey the wind will ice your back
and strip your grey hair from your balding head
Uncle! Where's your socks
your jandals will slip your feet wet
Uncle! Drink this coffee
to warm your chest in strength
Uncle! Try these trackpants
your lavalava will blow you down
Uncle! Where's your shoes
your size is nevermind
Uncle! Here's your money
don't give it to the church
Uncle! Stop phoning Samoa
the bill will reach the sky
Uncle! Don't plant those taro leaves
the flowers are for the mind
Uncle! Why do you sit there in the corner
night and day
Uncle! Where's your passport
NOW you've overstayed.

JOE BALAZ

Joe Balaz is a Hawaiian writer of Hawaiian, Slovakian and Irish descent. He writes in American English, Pidgin (Hawai'i Creole English) and creates concrete poetry (visual art poems). He edited *Ho'omānoa: An Anthology of Contemporary Hawaiian Literature*, and from 1980 to 1997 was the editor of *O'ahu Review*, a multicultural literary publication of Hawai'i. He is also the author and orator of *Electric Laulau*, a CD of his Pidgin writing set to music.

Moe'uhane

I dream of
the ways of the past –

I cannot go back.

I hike the hills
   and valleys of Wahiawā,
walking through crystal
            streams
      and scaling green cliffs.

I play in the waves
            of Waimea,
and spear fish
   from the reefs of Pāpa'iloa.

I grow bananas, 'ulu,
      and papayas,
   in the way of the 'āina.

I cannot go back –

I never left.

Huaka'i

Make strong the cord
        which binds the canoe,
    we are sailing home.

The storm
        which swamped
    our peaceful voyage
        is behind us now.

The wind lashed,
        the waves pounded,
    but we did not go down.

Make strong the cord
        which binds the canoe,
    we are sailing home.

Spear Fisher

In Kona
a Midwest businessman
        caught a marlin,
and hung it upside down
                on a wharf –

        At Hale'iwa
        I caught a kūmū,

                and I ate it.

Off Pōka'i Bay
a foreign competitor
        caught a tuna
and hung it upside down
                on a wharf –

        At Pāpa'iloa
        I caught an 'āweoweo,

                and I ate it.

Near Makapu'u
a thrill-seeking adventurer
         caught a shark,
and hung it upside down
                    on a wharf –

    At Pūpūkea
    I caught an āholehole,

         and I ate it.

In the fishing magazine
and the tournament boxscore,
egos reap the ocean of trophies –

On the North Shore of O'ahu,
I harvest a gift of life.

Da Last Squid

Willy Boy wen score.
On da mudflat
wheah da reef used to be,
he wen speah da buggah –
da last squid, brah.

In da abandoned conservation area
between da industrial park
and da old desalinization plant,
he wen find 'um,
dough how any squid
could live ovah deah,
I dunno –
Maybe da ting
wuz wun mutant, eh?

And as to how
Willy could go diving in dat spot
next to da effluent outflow,
I dunno eidah.
You know wat "effluent" mean, eh?
Dats just wun nice word foa dodo watah.

But still den,
Willy wuz all excited
aftah he wen cook dat squid.
Wen he wuz cutting 'um up
he wen tell me,

"Eh, you know wat dis is, eh?
Dis is da last squid, braddah!"

Da last squid –
It's kindah funny, brah,
wen I tink back,
but it really wuz da last squid.
Now by dat same beach
nutting can even live,
cause da watah stay all black
and even moa polluted den before.
It's just like tings wen change ovahnight.

But you know,
it started long time ago.
Way back wen,
I remembah my maddah told me,
just before I wuz born,
dey wuz building wun second city on Oʻahu
and finishing wun new tunnel on da windward side.

Latah on,
wen I wuz growing up
tings wen accelerate,
and da whole island
wen just develop out of control
into wun huge monstah city.

By den
had so many adah tunnels too,
dat da mountain
wen look like wun honeycomb.
Everyting came different, brah,
cause da island
wen grow so fast
and had so many people.

Maybe good ting Willy Boy wen make early –
He nevah live to see
how tings got even moa worse.

But back den,
wen we wuz youngah,
he looked so happy
wen he wuz cutting up dat contaminated he'e.
I can still heah his words –

"Dis is special, brah –
Dis is da last wun."

Wen he wen offah me some,
foa a lottah reasons
dats hard foa explain,
I just told 'um,

"Naay – No need – "

But deep inside, brah,
I nevah like be da wun to eat
da last squid.

KATHY BANGGO

Kathy Dee Kaleokealoha Kaloloahilani Banggo received a 1998 Elliot Cades Award for Literature presented by the Hawai'i Literary Arts Council, a national 1995 Intro Journal Award from the Associated Writing Programs, as well as a 1995 Hemingway Award and 1990 Myrle Clark Creative Writing Award from the University of Hawai'i. She has published a chapbook entitled *4-Evaz, Anna* by Tinfish Network, and her work has also appeared in *Hawai'i Review, Tinfish, La'iLai'i, Quarterly West*, and *Growing Up Local*. She works as a proofreader for a global CPA firm, and also as a freelance writer. She is Hawaiian-Filipino and was born in 1964 on the island of Oahu, Hawai'i. She is an avid surfer.

Mesmerism

Born she in the year of the mo'o,
in the time of love and war.

Returned she from the floating-on-the-back turtle
Honua to the dream time of Maui.

Watched was she in the light by Maui.
Watched was she in the dark by Maui.

Possessed he by the stone fire rivers of Pele.
Held fast she by the loin teeth of Maui.

From the wakeful sleep
caused he the spin of the earth

faster. He crept upon her.
The womb filled. The belly rounded.

Welcomed she the enduring waters.
Welcomed she the blanket of Po.

Thirst

for Kehuhaupi'o

Dry-eyed, you bring
your calabash of stones
up from the lower regions.

Brother, my skin is hollow.
My willow arms dangle
and I have lost my fragrance.

I am without water, or wet mouth
to kiss your thin lips into bloom,
to keep them from stinging.

All night while you wrestled the mo'o,
I watched from the inner valleys,
waiting for first light.

Listen: while we slept,
I loosened your warrior's braid
and brushed through the tangle of spirit,

the reluctant marriage of shadow and bones.
These carvings are locked in stone;
the petroglyphs dance, chanting their mute chant:

> *he pule no ka ua*

> *he pule no ka ua*

our bodies are gesture, a prayer for rain.

Bloom

Uncertain
this prayer

the unbraiding
of hands

palms surface
the quiet of the body

fingertips
a quiver of sacred flowers

feather the reef of the skin
breath like ocean whispers

damp
blue in spaces

Fly, Da Mo'o & Me

Befo time, I wuz bright.
But no mo now,
I stay stink.
I stay ugly.

      I used to be bright.
But then I walked up to him, where he sat weaving
ti leaves on the grass.
I wen tell em about my tutu and the kalo.

He blocked the doorway with his arms on both sides.
I no could get out.
         "Get on da bed," he wen tell me.
Only one window and a fly and a lizard high up on the wall.
I looked at the bed.
         "No scaid," he said.

Befo time, I wuz bright.
But no mo now,
I stay stink.
I stay ugly.

      I used to be bright.
But then he put the ti leaf around my neck.
I talked about my gramma and the kalo.

He shut the door and bolted it.
Wuz stuck.

"Take em in," he said from behind.

I nevah look.

"Come on, don't be afraid."

Up close to the fly, I count his wild eyes. Get planny. The mo'o
chirps, wiggles close and snap up my fren. Da fuckah burp.

Dey Wen Sen Me Girls' Home

cuz my bruddah got stab.
da punk wen sell my skateboahd
and his c.d. playah
fo some stuffs.
what is share?
bruddah shoot up all
himself. no mo fo me.
he try false crack me.

nobody wuz home dat time.
get ony us two. I like yell
"what, Mojo, gotta make big body?
eh, wuz mine one too",
but no could come out.
wuz stuck in my troat.
wuz shaking, like pilk.
What is can breathe?
"Black ass," bruddah said.
I wen poke em.

wuz e.z. da blood stay come out
da puka. he hol em two hands
by da stomach. only small da knife,
kine use fo cut da mango, pio da skin.
he wuz choking wen I call
da ambulanz. dey wen come
but he wuz pass out,
an my maddah wuz home
already. dey all ony good
fo stare.

"take em Kaneohe,"
my maddah wen point at me
"mento hospito.
dey put em strait jacket
geev em shock treatment."
I snob em, cuz her, she like
my bruddah mo bettah.
"go," I tell em, "go".

my calabash antie live nex doah
she alwayz weah da nice kine dress
get flowas; an she get 'ehu hair,
not oily an no mo flakes.
smell good her house. one time
she let me stan by da front porch
look insai, stay clean,
an no mo kakaroach
like ours one get
planny.

she wuz outsai da yahd
crying wen da police wen cuff me.
I wuz dying fo tell her
bruddah deserve his licks;
how he peep insai her window
wen her ole man no stay;
why he gotta make la dat fo?
how come he always
gotta jam me up
black ass bebe
bruddah tell me
he jealous I surf Ehu Kai.
bruddah dahk, too, ah
but he ony fake
he light.

CHERIE BARFORD

Cherie Barford was born in 1960 to a German-Samoan mother and a Palagi father. She writes when she can and has been published here and there, and in 2001 and 2002 she was a guest poet at the Going West literary festival in Auckland. A New Zealand Arts Council grant has enabled her to complete 'Westie File', a collection of poems which she hopes will be published soon. Cherie lives with her children in West Auckland and currently works as the Literacy Co-ordinator for Waitake Adult Literacy Inc.

Plea to the Spanish Lady

The people of Western Samoa were told that the sickness which eventually killed 22 per cent of their population after World War I was called "The Spanish Lady". This is one man's plea.

Important streets fall before you
and now   *Talune* berthed in Apia
harbours your sway
Sway not our way   Lady
Such homage grieves us

Aboard *Talune* the Doctor examines
bodies propped by mail bags
Colonel Logan agrees
                        "Yes,
a sea-sick lot this one."
The ocean is calm

Today the *Samoan Times* is all news:
death notices and a front page
Today the editor died
Today Teuuila's screams awoke me
as she lay between her parents
dipping fingers in their sweat

Her name means flower   Lady
see her tremble and wilt
We will bury her in lavalava
scented with frangipani

At Papauta Girls' School desks are empty
Colonel Logan shouts "I do not care if they
are going to die. Let them die and go to Hell."
American medicine is sent back unopened

He's never cared for us   Lady
He's not my brother in Christ   He can't be
Logs tumble, tumble from his eyes
Crosses bearing corpses swim in them
My flesh is moist   too moist
Who will harvest the taro and breadfruit?
Who will instruct the young?   Feed my children?

Don't linger Spanish Lady
The trenches are full and
my family spills into the ocean
fevered and dazed
drowning at each other's feet
Go now   Lady
We have fallen before you

Eclipse Friday 23 November 1984

The radio told New Zealand
not to look at the sun

while my mother scrubbed
the shower-box
                quickly
so she wouldn't miss the eclipse

Sharon rang to say
that Southland was flooding
though the sky looked great
through strips of negative film

and interrupted the chapter on reprisals
                              The part where
women with shaven heads were dragged
naked through liberated streets

while boys with gouged eyes went insane
because insects were sewn into the wounds

My God   How can people?   How can people . . . ?

I skipped the details to find
that the dead woman was identified
                              hours later
by a grieving husband who recognised her shoes
                                        nothing else

and wondered why my friend who
loved women and painted their moods
had given me the book saying
                              You must read it

Feeling disturbed I rose
to switch on the lights
because the day had turned dull
while my mother mopped the floor
                              snapping my fingers
at her expression

See – History happens all the time
The moment is gone yet memories remain

and she laughed   saying
Isn't it eerie?

as I remembered a man swimming
from a cave into an equator sun

Hi
I'm a Kiwi
Where are you from?
He'd replied distinctly –
My mother is French
My father was a German soldier
                              as if it really mattered

and I discovered much later
that details really do

Under a darkening sky
I thought of this beautiful man
and our vulnerable love
in my twenty-second summer

I'd never asked if his mother
had been dragged through streets
because his voice was soft
when he spoke of her
and that was my answer

One day I'd cried
because I felt he adored me
for my name
              which stirred
some remembrance within him
when he loved me
So silly yet so real

The postcard of a village
in Alsace-Lorraine
                    still looks picturesque

though we stopped writing
after two years
                          and

today as the sun eclipses
I imagine him married
with gorgeous children

Wondering what our child
could have looked like

as I've done countless times
since he kissed into my hair
                              the image of

a babe with my skin
your hair and eyes
our smile

I'd known that only
a wife who would stay
forever could have his child

and promises are useless
when you're unsure

But right now
on this eclipsed day
the moments seem precious
the memories are mine

and my mother is all excited
because she saw the darkness

AUDREY BROWN

Born in Rarotonga, Cook Islands in July 1975, Audrey Teuki Tetupuariki Tuioti Brown is of Cook Island Maori and Samoan descent. She has a BA in sociology and political studies and is currently a diplomat with the Cook Islands High Commission in New Zealand. She was the writer for the short film *The Cat's Crying*, screened on TVNZ's Tagata Pasifika programme in 1995, and assisted in the production of the experimental film *The Rainbow* in 1997–98. Her poetry was included in an exhibition catalogue produced by the Australian Centre for Photography in 1998 and in the 2002 New Zealand Fringe Festival performance, *The Past with the Present: Teuki*, joint winner of the Festival's Spoken Word Award. In 2002 Audrey's first collection of poetry, with the visual images and design of Cook Island artist Veronica Vaevae, was published by Steele Roberts in *Threads of Tivaevae: Kaleidoskope of Kolours*.

local tourist on a bus ride home

cool breeze sweeping sweet sweat of sadness
(through the cold hot air of the open closed window)

look   "sweet-e"
                not with your i i dar-ling

?   (anonymous object sits silently inside palm of her head)

the mist kisses the mountains
the mountains kiss the sky
                coloured pockets of green & gold & blue
                sing her a familiar song she thought she could never understand

(fault?)   *Tuatua maori*   *no*
                       church   *no*
                       hula   *kare?*

echoed an even more familiar voice inside her head 2 herself
                                        the bird flies over the sun
                                        the sun flies in2 the sea

thoughts (r) / evolve as the km (s) clock from papa joe's watch & the o-do-me-ter
of the yellow – yellow/jam packed/yellow/jam packed bus

(on the ½ hr anti-clock-wise of course)

10   9   8   7   6   5   4   ………………………………...............

watch the c   through the trees
                                                     through the houses

through the stones that paint each stop with a story of a somebody
a n d   a   s o m e w h e r e   t h a t   a   s o m e o n e (s)   s t i l l   l o v e s …………………..

can u c

as they pass her-story in arorangi & tupapa…………..

o'er dose on the self-indulgence of self-importance

self-importance embossed with kluttony & aka-aka-day-me-a
slashed with a few latin letters
left right centre   mainly right

              pride   watching mamas clean your house ?
                                 as my little kirls say   no way man!
                                                                           no way!
the virtues of maoridom   (virtu as in man)

"if you want 2 know how 2 speak the language   *MY DEAR*
get yourself a maori poyfriend who can speak maori"

tuatua maori   dependent upon the vowel sounds of
                                                                   tane
                                                                   virtu
                                                                   tane ?

please   y he look at people with disdain?

                                here he goes again …………………….

"government policy   (he thought upon non-re-flec-tion)
                                we only employ maori who speak maori?"

$14,000 + 47,000 = \%?$

ethnicity defined on one premise –

fuck   u one lousy aka-dem-ick?

mother land so good have to find
new father land of bastardised kulcha
under flag of polygamist state

the dizzy-land of poly-nesia inc.

fly the flag at half-mast
cause when he goes what a loss it will be

yeah whatever?
not   not   not   she says   (again & again & again)

as the ad on the visually impaired box says to her & everybody else all amazingly at once

ka kite!

he says / she says   *sad arse truth MY DEAR*   *is*

i is right.

big game fishing wearing the joker's tea cup

confusion laced in like & lust & sweat & alcohol plenty

he says all the time 2 himself
1 4 for the road again & again & again

"i don't care who you r (?)"

stomps the box in the corner
& in another space as she sits past time in her office
the same is repeated in the floor of the post office
of the blue-ly uniformed posties who sort out the mail

(trying 2 play cool like she don't care)
the need 2 be wanted supersedes
a gentle hand unmasks secrets
looks......lingering looks & touch   (change the subjec t)
                                         hmmmm?...................

the secret codes of pseudo-partners   was & the computer
                                           tormented fisherman & the charming alcoholic

in the search to find the value of xy................
                                           she wakes 2 find herself alone
                                         monday 2 friday, friday 2 friday

she looks 2 the mountains that sit outside her window
listening 2 herself she tries 2 silence her thoughts

accident happens –   manwalk falls
                                         bang on ground
                                         play-retry-play

                                       volume?

fuck no more music!

ALISTAIR TE ARIKI CAMPBELL

Alistair Te Ariki Campbell, poet, playwright and novelist, was born in 1925 in Rarotonga in the Cook Islands and spent his first seven years there. His mother was a Penrhyn Islander and his father a third-generation New Zealander from Dunedin. For years, Campbell was a poet in the European tradition. The first major expression of his early Polynesian influences was in *Sanctuary of Spirits* (1963), when he chose to write of the Maori history which surrounded his home at Pukerua Bay, near Wellington. At that time he identified with the local Ngāti Toa tribe but later he returned to the Cook Islands and found a new sense of identity. His publications of poetry include *Kapiti* (Pegasus Press, 1972), *The Dark Lord of Savaiki* (Te Kotare Press, 1980), *Soul Traps* (Te Kotare Press, 1985), *Stone Rain: The Polynesian Strain* (Hazard Press, 1992), *Pocket Collected Poems* (Hazard Press, 1996), *Maori Battalion: A Poetic Sequence* (Wai-te-ata Press, 2001), a sequence of poems that takes the reader into the minds of the soldiers in the Maori Battalion, and his latest work, *Poets in Our Youth: Four Letters in Verse* (Pemmican Press, 2002), one of which is addressed to James K. Baxter.

Te Hura

Some say that Kavariki,
            the most beautiful of women,
                        invented the dance.
I say it was Kavariki
            and Urerua together.
                        When her pubic hairs
were as fine as mouse-down,
            none had removed her
                        pareu except her mother.
When they turned wiry,
            it was the High Priest
                        Urerua who preformed
the initiation rite.
            With his double-size phallus
                        he discovered te hura
in the split-drum of her
            belly, whence flowed
                        the genius of our people . . .
Urerua and Kavariki
            revered for their inventiveness.

Maui's Whare

Maui hauled it up from the sea.
     His fish-hook caught it
          by a window-frame,
and when he landed it
     the structure was askew.
          But the strange thing was
an old man and his wife
     and daughters were still
          in residence: four pairs
of eyes stared out at him,
     utterly astonished,
          but not as much as he.
He scowled, took up the whare
     and shook it angrily
          until the old man and
his family fell screaming
     through the doorway
          and smashed their brains out
on the rocks of Kura Passage
     fifty feet below.
          Thereupon, with infinite care,
the mischief-maker
     took up the broken bodies
     and tried to breathe life
into their gaping mouths,
     but their spirits had already
          fled to Te Po,
squeaking with indignation.
     Then Maui put the house down
          tried to straighten it,
failed and went away.

Solomona

To die is simply to walk
     away from the body
          without regret or pain,
and with no thought of
     turning back, for there is
          nothing to turn back to,

except the empty shell
           that relatives weep over.
                   I have often left
my body here at Te Tautua,
           crossed the lagoon and
                   walked among my sleeping
kinsfolk at Omoka to see
           if all was well.
                   My family know my door
must be kept open
           if I am to rejoin my body,
                   but sometimes through
carelessness they have
           almost shut me out.
                   Now it is time to go,
to walk the steep track
           to Savaiki alone. I have
                   enjoined my dear ones
to close the door firmly
           after me, when I leave
                   on my last visit to Omoka.
They weep, but will obey.

Tangaroa

Old friend and fellow voyager,
           don't say I didn't warn you.
                   It was different in the old days
when you and I and Seimata
           roamed the world as champions.
                   It was Seimata who peeled off
the eight skins of the sky
           and revealed the bloodied
                   godhead of Rorangi,
and you who met the challenge
           of the great sea serpent
                   that had coiled itself
and swallowed its tail
           within the ancient
                   navel of Tongareva.
It was I who learned,
           at the feet of Ataranga,

to build ancestral song.
Sleep was ever good to us,
      and when we ventured out
         upon the waters of Kare
the peace that fell on us
      stretched all the way to Savaiki.
         Now, old friend, it's time to go.
Our ocean-going double canoe
      awaits us, stocked for the voyage.
         Our men are seated and,
as we embark, they shout and raise
      their paddles to salute us.
         We can delay no longer.

Tongareva

Listen to the moon, young people.
      She talks to the fish,
         she talks to the sperm
the salmon of the body.
      The moon knows better than you
         when to make love,
when to abstain from making love.
      The moon rests her chin
         on the horizon and tells you,
young women, to prepare your nets,
      to get them ready for the night
         of mating that awaits you.
Now the moon rises from the sea,
      streaked with blood,
         and calls to the fish.
And, young men, though you use line
      and hook, don't expect success
         to be other than testing.
As for you, young women, evade
      the hook, do not yield
         easily, evade the hook.
This is the night most favourable
      for a fine catch, so get up,
         young girls, and shake
the dreams out of your hair, float
      your bodies on the incoming tide

and open your legs, face
the moon boldly. I say, open
    your nets for the fish to enter.
        The fish know where to go.
They evade the hooks, swimming
    in wide circles – the night fish,
        the fish that know the depths
and rise to the moon's exultation,
    following the singing to its source
        to die in the eclipse.
The moon will then withdraw,
    and the tide, too, will withdraw
        through rents in the reef.
Beware, then, of the stone fish
    skulking in the shallows.
        One false step, young women,
and you will lose all the fish
    you gathered in your nets.
        Let the young men withdraw,
but not too soon, leaving you scarred.
    Let them try once more
        for a bigger and better prize.
Just as Maui broke his nose
    with his fist, baited his hook
        with his blood, and raised
Tongareva from the depths,
    so, young men, do likewise,
        and the fish will return,
shimmering in their thousands –
    the big fish, the small fish,
        the fish with gaping mouths
that lie in the reef channels.
    Young women, young girls,
        the trap-pockets in your nets
will not be strong enough
    to hold the swarming fish –
        the mesh will give way
and the fish will escape.
    And so learn to draw
        the string that closes the net –
and be contented with your catch.
    The retreating tide will hum
        its tune of contentment,
swirling out between your toes.

So be contented with your catch.
            If you wake too soon,
before the fish have spawned,
            acknowledge your failure –
                  you are not disgraced.
It's necessary to be humble
      if you wish to succeed
            in your final attempt.
If you fail again, young girls,
      the moon will die within you,
            and yours will be the shallows
the turtles never revisit.
      So try again, exercising
            the utmost patience as the moon,
singing through its quarters,
      comes back renewed.
            And don't be afraid when joy
goes rushing through your veins
      tearing new rents
            in the reef, but believe
in your good fortune that you
      may never again experience.
            This time take up a net
as delicate as it is strong,
      and make sure as before
            the mouth faces the shallows,
for then the fish will spawn
      and as they seek to escape
            to the open sea, trap them
in the net and close the mouth.
      You may despise your men
            with their crude line and hook,
but you may need their hands
      to hold the net steady.
            Afterwards, if no longer useful,
you can always eat them.
      But above all, young women,
            be patient, for if you close
your net too soon, you may lose
      your catch, and the moon
            that presided over your birth
will set on your dreams,
      and you will know the bitterness
            of having lost Tongareva.

Absence

I never eat sensibly when you're away.
I make do with odd scraps of food
that don't need heating up,
or nibble on a biscuit or two.
Under the pine trees
the dogs wait through wind and rain
for your return.

I fiddle with a poem,
searching for a true rhyme,
but settle for less.
If it gets any colder I may light a fire,
or I may not.
I take up a book of poems,
but after a few pages I put it down.

Far away the sea climbs the road
that you have taken,
and lazily climbs down,
leaving a white smear.
Under low mist and rain,
Kapiti drifts towards Australia.
It will be another long day
before you return.

Roots

The wind blew hard again today,
tried to blow away my poems,
but to no avail,
for they had sunk their roots
deep into the hillside,
deep into the stones, the grass,
the trees, the songs of birds,
the light on land and sea
that never dies,
the light in your eyes.

Jock Campbell my Father

Yes, I remember the transport *Southland* –
a tub of a ship with a contingent
of Aussie larrikins, and a few of us
from the other side of the ditch –
real New Zealanders, and proud of it.
We found their boasting pretty hard to take.
Then a torpedo struck us amidships
and the blast knocked me unconscious.
I floated to the surface, entangled
with ropes and every kind of debris.
What an approach to the Dardanelles!
There was not a sign of a ship –
only an oil slick, bilge, torn uniforms,
naked bodies, dead horses, and men
clinging to spars and planks, and cursing,
real blister-raising curses from the Aussies.
We had our differences, but you can't
help liking men who rush into battle
yelling *Imshi Tallah*, a cry picked up
in a Cairo street. The legend that we share
was born when our joint forces fought
and died together in Anzac Cove . . .
I am lying in Tahiti with my dear Teu.
It's quiet here away from the guns, the screams,
the nightmare that was Gallipoli. I can't
make out what she is murmuring, but I think
it's about forgetfulness and peace.

Stretcher-bearer

I see them still, cursing the generals
who put them in this spot – the incompetent
generals who sent them to their death.
Over the top was the cry,
and they went over and were slaughtered.
The Turk was scarcely better off,
but at least he occupied the heights
and look down on us, while we

looked up, blinded by dust and blood.
The stink of the unburied dead
was always in our nostrils.
We drank that stink, we ate it
with our bully beef, we breathed it.
There was nothing over the top
but death. I lost my best mates
on the cliffs of Gallipoli. They cry out
to me still, but I can no more
help them now than I could then.

Gallipoli Peninsula

It was magical when flowers
appeared on the upper reaches –
not that we saw much of the upper reaches.
But when we did,
we were reminded of home
when spring clothed the hills with flowers.
The dead lying among them
seemed to be asleep.
I can never forget the early mornings,
before the killings started up,
when the sea was like a mirror
under little wisps of cloud
breathing on its surface, so dazzling
it hurt the eye.
And the ships, so many of them,
they darkened the sea.
But the evenings too were magical,
with such hues in the sky
over Macedonia,
so many colours, gold bars,
green, red, and yellow.
We noticed these things,
when the firing stopped and we had respite.
It was good to feel,
during such moments,
that we were human beings once more,
delighting in little things
in just being human.

Tohi

Kia ora. We understand these things. We are
    warriors still. No longer is tohi practised –
        and more's the pity. But the fighting man
performs the rituals in his heart and guts.
    When Death sings in his hair and crackles
        to his fingertips he becomes fully alive.
Darkness overcomes him and flames rush
    before his eyes. We answered the call to arms –
        men from Te Arawa and Ngati Porou,
men from Ngati Kahungunu, men from all
    the iwi, from Aupouri in the north,
        to Ngaitahu in the south. We had our
nicknames – The Gumdiggers, The Penny Divers,
    The Cowboys, and The Foreign Legion, later
        Ngati Walkabout. As the war raged on,
from Greece to Crete, to North Africa, to Italy,
    we all truly belonged to Ngati Walkabout.
        And everywhere we fought, the long tongues
of our bayonets, having tasted human flesh,
    hungered for more. We fed our bayonets
        on German flesh. They rejoiced in the whana
tukutahi, the mad charge, the terror,
    the sexual thrust into flesh, the screams.
        Tumatauenga glared over our shoulders
yelling, 'Kill them!' until our bayonets were sated,
    and the dead lay steaming like a hangi,
        when kaitangata was the warrior's just reward.

Sergeant Jack Tainui

The river was swift and shallow,
    and noting that the enemy could
        make the crossing by leaping
from rock to rock, and being then
    at their most vulnerable
        to surprise attack, Major Dyer
sent me to observe and take
    whatever action I thought
        necessary to prevent the enemy

succeeding. I slid down the hill,
      concealing myself where I could,
         until I gained the river bank
and when they began to cross over
      I waited until the leading group
         had got halfway, then opened fire,
killing three, and in the panic
      that followed I shot the fourth.
         I watched as he crawled away,
took aim to finish him off,
      but found I couldn't do it.
         He may have died anyway.

Green Lizards

Mountainous country, deep wooded
      gorges, villages clinging
         to cliffsides by a fingernail,
waterfalls and swift streams,
      ancient olive trees, a gritty
         people generous with the little
they have, rain that never stops –
      this was Greece to us. Sometimes
         the roads cut through forests
for logging trucks reminded us
      of the Urewera, and when we saw
         men and women gathering puha
and fishshops selling kina,
      we knew we had come a long way
         to find people like ourselves.
Here, lizards are green, and we
      took them for good omens, until
         the sky fell on us. We grew
eyes on the back of our heads from
      retreating. Sneaking off in the night
         is not the way to run a war.

Captain H. W. Leaf

Now there was a man, big in every way,
        a big heart, big in body, a great fighter.
                He was the stuff that legends are made of.
He was talked about whenever and wherever
        his former comrades got together.
                He didn't die in the normal way.
No bullet can kill a legend. He goes on
        living in men's hearts, inspiring, leading,
                setting an example of courage that never
surrenders. We knew the legend, how he had
        taken to the hills where he was training
                a loyal band of followers for the attack
that would drive the enemy from the island,
        and we wanted to believe it. We knew
                the official account of his death, how
he had led his company, unwittingly,
        beyond the start-line of an attack,
                and was killed crossing a bridge,
but the real part of him, his legend,
        lives on, whether his name is known or not.
                He lives in the hills rallying the dead.

Westward

The sun is setting, laying
        a quivering path to the sea
                for the dead to follow.
They have waited for the wind to
        abate and the aircraft
                and warships to move away.
Now it is safe to be going.
        There's a sound of sighing
                as they part from their
bodies and take to the air,
        and along both fronts
                the living are afraid.

Desert Flower

He was shot in the backside
      as he bent to pick
            a flower, and as he lay
dying, he thought of the
      joke, "He must have been
            running away", but it
didn't seem funny
      any more. The flower
            was tiny, like a spot
of blood when a finger
      is pricked, like the glint
            in a moth's eye, like
his mind that had shrunk
      to a point of light,
            winking as it went out.

Death of a Friend

Friend, you died at Florence,
      tragically close to war's end.
            We crawled through a minefield
to escape Jerry's net. I got
      through safely, but a land mine
            blew off your leg. I heard you
cursing horribly, calling down
      every possible evil on the evildoers
            who had done this to your leg,
and you used a belt as a tourniquet
      to stop the bleeding, but your life
            flowed away, and I heard
your spirit wailing as it flew
      over my head, seeking faraway Reinga.
            You had just turned twenty-two.

To Stuart

Early spring, and a cold wet morning.
        The wind mooches about outside,
                planning a home invasion.
It's Mary's birthday, our Mary whom
        you'd have loved had the Fates
                spared you. I take you back
five years before you joined
        the Maori Battalion, and six before you
                died. I have many questions to put
to you, many that may not even have
        an answer. Why being blessed with
                enviable gifts did you abandon
your studies after only a year?
        You could have made your mark
                in any field that calls
for passion and imagination.
        As a boy I followed you about
                from match to match marvelling
at what you created with a
        cricket ball. Your bowling
                action and the flight of the ball,
gathering speed as it flew
        towards its target, were to me
                a work of art. As an admiring
younger brother, I celebrate
        this image of what you promised
                and never lived to fulfil.
'Nature,' wrote William Blake,
        'has no Outline, but Art has.'
                I see you turn and run up
to the crease. I see your
        arm swing over. I see the
                ball in flight – and that is all.

JACQ CARTER

Jacq Carter's first appearance in print was in Witi Ihimaera's *Growing Up Maori* in 1998, a collection of diverse opinion on what it is to "grow up Maori". Jacq's somewhat lengthy tirade (her own choice of words!) was accompanied by four of her poems, one of which appears here, "Powhiri". Jacq is now 28 years old and enjoying a change of pace with her lovely little son, Te Whaiti-nui-a-Toi Te Reke, born December 2001.

At the end of our road

You can look out over
Takaparawha
synonymous with the struggle
of Ngati Whatua
you can just make out
the tekoteko
standing at the head
of Tumutumuwhenua

It is black
even against Rangitoto's flanks
and speaks to me of stories burned
Okahu Bay in the 1950s
the whare itself in 1990
the year they celebrated
the "birth of a nation"
the "spirit of the Treaty"
bi-culturalism

It always looks peaceful
from the end of our road
as if no little girl
ever lost her life
as if five hundred and six days
didn't end in police violence
as if victories won
can't be undone

Bastion Point
I hope they can't

Comparatively Speaking, There is No Struggle

When people like you tell me

things aren't as bad here
as they are elsewhere

I wish you had been there

in the Waikato
or amongst my own people

the century before last
and every day after that

standing on land
that is no longer yours
fishing from waters
that no longer run pure

or at every hui
on every marae
that activates the words
mana Maori motuhake

which is every marae in the country.

You seem to think things
are better off here
because you don't see us dying
or visibly fighting

as if it all happened
in yesteryears.

I tend to think

that one of the worse effects of
colonisation

is when people no longer fight
because they don't see a need
and think that

comparatively speaking
everything's alright.

So how many Maori
have you convinced today
that really us "Mahrees"
should consider ourselves lucky
that things could have been worse
as they are with the "Abos"?

Me aro koe ki te hā o Hineahuone!

If Hinetītama
can become Hinenuitepo

crushing

the next man that tried to interfere with her
between her thighs

then I too can deal to any man
that would enter me without my permission.

If our tipuna wahine
can have the courage and the vision

to leave their homelands
in search of new homes

then I too can leave any place
that does not nourish and support me.

If that great ancestress Wairaka
can summon the strength of any man

and drag that waka
from the sea to land

then I shall not allow myself
let alone anyone else
to think of me as less
than his or her equal.

This is what we mean
when we speak of mana wahine

we carry it in our breath
by virtue of our descent from Hineahuone

which is why when you meet a woman
you really ought to hongi

to pay heed
to the strength
that is women.

E tū, e tū, e tū, Tānemahuta!

Twenty-three years
is a long time to live
without ever seeing a kauri

. . .

Seeing you now
both saddens
and angers me

all I can do is hongi

twice

for the greatness of you
and the absence of more of you

. . .

When I grow old

I hope to stand
as tall as you do

and to have lots of mokopuna
to plant more of you.

For a tipuna wahine

Ani Mereti Rihara
are you my kaitiaki now?

Now when I am trying
to tell the world who you are
and that I descend from you?

I'm imagining you now, e kui

a bit like these women
I see on the street

great women these

with strength enough
to hold future generations.

Ani Mereti Rihara
you are telling me who I am

when I am white as the eyes
they judge me with each day

no regard for the woman
who had blood enough for me.

E kui,

they mapped your proud descent
then ignored it as theirs

only a name to them
but you live and breathe in me.

I am
because you were

and because I am
you are.

Aroha

I gave to you a rock
from which you built a wall
then you stood there at the top
making me feel small

I gave to you a seed
from which you grew a tree
then you told me all its fruit
did not belong to me

kss kss auē hā

I took you to a mountain
you did not want to climb
instead you tunnelled deep inside
for treasures that were mine

I led you to the ocean
and taught you about the tides
now I go down to the shore
and all the fish have died

kss kss auē hā

I told you all my stories
you wrote down every word
now I find my stories
are no longer to be heard

I carved a piece of greenstone
and hung it round your neck
then you made a thousand more
only yours were made of plastic

kss kss auē hā

I gave birth to a daughter
a child for you and me
but you did all the parenting
so she wouldn't turn out like me

Then I signed your piece of paper
some kind of guarantee
that while you would watch over them
these things belonged to me

kss kss auē hā

I gave to you kāwanatanga
a kind of governing
but I didn't give you mana
because there's mana in being me

I embrace my own uniqueness
my rangatiratanga too
I will have the rights that you have
without having to be like you

kss kss auē hā

And one day I will walk again
the lands you stole from me
only this time I'll be standing tall
and Papatūānuku will be free

Pōwhiri

My sadness is
I have never known
a kuia fold me
in her arms

My sadness is
that what I know
was not told me
by my kaumatua

My sadness is
that I don't have the reo
that what I feel
can't be fully told

but I hear the call of my tupuna
the strongest karanga I know

I bow my head
with respect for them
and from them I draw strength
they walk with me
as I take my first steps
towards all that is theirs

ka tangi te titi
ka tangi te kākā
ka tangi hoki ahau
Tihei mauri ora!

ki ngā mate kua haere ki te pō
ka tangihia e ahau i tēnei wā

haere, haere, haere atu ra.

SAMUEL CRUICKSHANK

Samuel Cruickshank writes that he is "a Maori-Scots kid who was conceived in Christchurch, gestated in Tonga and eventually surfaced in Labasa, Fiji".

urban iwi: tihei mauri ora!

bound together by mobile phones
we kōrero our brown words
through fibre-optic, satellite networks
of tukutuku DNA.

daily, our moko spirals are served
to us in coffee cups of ground
dark beans, infused with
milky, swirling froth

with bums on seats, we gather kūmara,
ika, oysters, kūtai and organic watercress
from menus at restaurants on Ponsonby Rd.

we navigate our paths in waka
that are power-steering pulled
through High St seas of suits and ties.

the city is our marae; skyscraper
tekoteko with a hundred square eyes
surround us on all sides.

at night, our people climb the sky tower
maunga and offer their koha
in karakia rituals of chance.

we email each other @www.flashmaori.co
fingers playing the pūtōrino on keyboards
of corporate hardware –
            – there is not an adze in sight.
only, the taiaha of new technologies
used skilfully in brown hands.

Sky Digital offers up images of our haka,
chanting its close-up shots of All Black
                                Te Rauparahas.
we lost the World Cup, and Hinewehi
Mohi could not sing our anthem in te reo
on a global satellite stage.

for waiata, we reach for our stereo remotes.
Mai FM 88.6, CDs – Oceania, Moana,
Betty Anne, Bic, Boh, & Kiri for a bit of an aria.
we hit the random button, and our people's songs
segue into Riki, Jennifer, Shania and
                                Robbie Williams.

there is a political swing towards removing
The Treaty. The Beehive is an uncontested site
for Maori Sovereignty –
                – it was a book once.
now it sits on the backbenches obscured
                by darkened spectacles.

and "we who sit in darkness" –
                – do we ride the crest of a new millennium?
who will be our Kupe next?

urban iwi, may we rise up and be counted.
may our voices be heard in this whenua,
                                that is Our home.
may we pull the mana of our tupuna from
within our globalised selves, and breathe again.

Tihei Mauri Ora! There is life within us!

Black Arse

The flash whare on the hill
is where we are today.
        A couple of "horis",
walking around on Indian
        sandstone floors
in an Italian lit castle.

Cher, not bad alright!
      This doesn't feel like
we're a
      "dying breed"
             to me.

Unless
      we've died
and gone to heaven,
           eh kare?

We raise our crystal goblets
To our delicate
          ngutu lips
And say "cheers black
          arse, take that!"

Pakiri: Midnight Sea

Where the orange moon
is silently strong

Rising like a fiery tonsil
from throat of sea.

Here, in this place
      of beauty,
Where the midnight
      landscape
holds her breath,
And gasps with want of
           words.

Here, in this place, I rest
and sit on cedar decked stage
hugging my knees
which hold my throat.

As my breath leaves my
chest, and rises with the
Lungs of the moon.

DAVID EGGLETON

David Eggleton's mother is Rotuman and his father is Pakeha; he was born in Auckland in 1952. He is a poet, writer and critic, and his publications include *South Pacific Sunrise* (poems, Penguin, 1986), *People of the Land* (poems, Penguin, 1988), *Empty Orchestra* (poems, AUP, 1995) and *After Tokyo* (short stories, E. S. A. W., 1987). His latest poetry collection, *Rhyming Planet*, was published by Steele Roberts in 2001. David lives in Dunedin, New Zealand.

The Werewolf of Grafton Gully

I have seen the best minds of my generation
teased by computers,
done up by *Miami Vice* leisurewear
in the wine bar dives of new Ponsonby,
worshipping art deco hamburgers enshrined on almighty altars
of junk food wrappers. Rising sons of Samoa's
old running shoes toe-tapping to an unchained melody
of shake, rattle and roll jewellery.
Seen holidays at Ruatoria in a Rastafarian theme park.
All our charismatic Christmases nowadays bearing witness
to rapid-rotate rotisserie rock-star corpses
done to a turn by the executive arm of the President
of Random Wipeout Facility Limited
on behalf of United Sugardaddies of America Incorporated.
Give me the massed sun umbrellas of the Waitemata,
the no-obligation mantras of the waves,
as one of the more thrusting big names strides through
the foam sweet foam,
mini-tanker under one arm and a copy of *the bone people*
under the other.
Behind plates of mirror-glass, a written-out write-off does his nut,
goes bananas, cops a case of kumara, and punches
a recurring rewrite of *This is Your Life* into a word processor,
rising from the crash barrier towards the steel wheels of a vacancy,
in the groovy ruts of the road on the street where I live,
stuck inside a parade of mobile homes,
drunk in charge of a test tube,
with some fishfingers thrust down my throat.
The shops are full of rubber gloves

and suction cups which have lost their suck.
This way to the jumble sales of dirty overcoats, to the shock-horror
billboards dealing in barbed-wire love, on the edge of the very rich
scum, the high tide of human kind, studied by body-climbing
profile shots,
stop-gap cover-ups and lipstick-coated heavyweights, who watch
a lettuce
wilt on video for the McDonald-murderburger-grubmerchants-to-
the-globe,
wired worldwide in Auckland, would-be home of the Auckland
Airport Massacre in B minor.
Behold this landscape of a thousand cocktails, where sometimes
can be seen
the lesser-spotted gum-chewers of Seattle and Chicago,
their Adidas footwear woven out of dollar bills,
each of them pursuing a meaningful relationship
with boogie-woogie,
burlesque queens of yesteryear along for the ride.
Bring on the nuclear-free lunch of Mr Banana Skins
and his transformer robots,
because I have seen this computer-generated generation stampede
the admass barricades of bubblegum, storm the seven veils
of wet Kleenex,
send a Cadillac into orbit, put a man on a liferaft,
and build an MX missile factory on Ronnie's Ranch.
Pull up to the bumper, baby, bump it to a trumpet, baby,
take the mainframe to Turkey, baby, culture vultures come closer,
you can wind me up, I'm a clockwork wally,
a walking suspended-animation zombie,
a Moriori voodoo dolly,
a living communications-network in designer jeans,
heading nowhere in a front-row bucket-seat and one-way mirror
shades,
the werewolf on Radio Howl,
the werewolf of Grafton Gully.
So, get down in the graveyard and dig it, dig it, dig it!

Republic of Fiji

Fringed by salt-water lace, the abandoned ship
British Empire drifts through Isles of Amnesia,
awaiting colonial mutual evaluation.

A shell roars inside the sea, calling to islands,
and islands surface like turtles in the rain:
rain white as mosquito net, white as grated coconut,
white as the helmets of ex-Governors-General.
Rain white like the walls of Suva city jail
walls which hold bloody hibiscus, bruised mango,
and crims who blow smoke at a dead volcano.

Orchids nod to sermons of the wet season;
jungle is green ink bleeding into sludge.
Rain erases the movie of "the great outdoors":
that soaked brouhaha of palm-trees threshing
in a mare's nest of tradewind tales and trails,
as coconuts arc like basketballs for the hoop,
woven baskets, tropical plunder steaming.
Today's colour bar is scar joining scar to scar,
while anthill streets relay a taboo beat to
the black swish of Ratu Sir Lala Sukuna's sulu.

Suva's sweatshop sews all into one sharkskin
when call of Shark-god pounding grog begins.
Muddy kava slurped up from a coconut bowl
drives us further into earth at each small go.
It is land-divers free-falling to Pentecost;
it is skull-binders bound for Vanuatu;
it is rafts of pumice fragments floating to Fiji;
it is a World War Two submarine still undersea,
its encrusted fire coral and brain coral battery
lighting up the Pacific with republican dreams.

The red eye of the Cobra coil burns to nothing.
Degei spits a gob of gold into the sky over Nadi,
and knocks heads of gods together, sucks out sap.
He shoulders a coconut sack, walks to market,
as if hauling an island along the sea's horizon.
Around reefs black and white sea-snakes spiral.
The bula boys' shirts are prayer flags in neon;
their thatch roof a top hat; Krishna's bus their chariot,
carrying them on firewheels whose spokes are knives,
along dirt roads where cane fields escalate into fire.

Maungapohatu 1916

A black Union Jack flutters in the photograph,
their features swim out towards you.
Light gropes along gullies,
Death's Cenotaph awaits the Last Quake.

The Crown held the land and
vapour trails of Empire wreathed
her blue triumphal arch which dims now
like the glow from autumn leaves.

Sunk in a polished black dawn, the prophet,
when nails ripped from his yawning house,
felt pushing in from the sea the wind,
smashing up off a skating silver sea.

Black mud slicked handcuffed hands,
his hair was a tangled alphabet.
Horse hooves clacked like skulls,
the barbed wire harp was strung and would sing.

Karangahape Road Celebrates

mango skin jewels Tahitian sunset rose and lime
earth-oven steam, punga moon, hibiscus sky
a summer frock that floats as she moves
a truckload of drumhead cabbages brakes to a halt
yams, boxes of wriggly pink toes
fat green banana fingers hula their way through slats
in a boarding house Monday stews away in a burnt saucepan
the gullies one long black mid-afternoon yawn
guava hangs on the air, frangipani too like sea-foam lace
cherry stains the purple lamingtons de luxe
through windows and cellophane
an instamatic cheeseburger snaps its garter . . .

Gulf Takeaways

A Hercules shadows the sunblown Hauraki.
Promenaders wheel bikes along the waterfront,
homeward-wending workers punt cars to the lights.
Plucked golden skin is ravaged in a burger bar,
hot oils rainbow a fried-chicken sunset.
Warp daily into the experience of a lifetime,
to be lost among the lukewarm slot machines!
Inside, sad tropicals play Space Invaders,
outside, bleached programmers topple into snow-white surf.
A dark child gathers a beachball of light against arms and ribs.
This monsoon-season sky
buds stars on its mango bloom.
Tree orchid scent sends the air crazy.
The face of the Gulf God spills upwards
to kiss the scraps of black waves coming down again.

Prime Time

The sun loves hot February to death,
girls do the hula till they're out of breath.
Youths on beaches are flinging frisbees.
Chaps in board shorts strut the Bee's Knees.
A tiara of lights on the Harbour Bridge,
a Cockroach Democracy behind the fridge.
Gross Crazies of the Junkosphere
are doing the backstroke through their beer.
Spiderman dangles from the lampshade,
a plastic goldfish swims in lemonade.
Civilisation smoked down to the filtertip.
Jehovah in a cloudburst would mean abandon ship.
Coronary bypass drunks pilot cannibal cars,
pursuing their own Paradises, Xanadus, Shangri-Las.

RANGI FAITH

Rangi Faith was born in Timaru, New Zealand in 1949 and is of Kāi Tahu descent. He is a teacher by profession and currently lives in Rangiora. He was the co-winner of the 1993 Te Atairangikaahu Commemorative Literary Award (for poetry), has edited a collection of poetry for New Zealand high schools entitled *Dangerous Landscapes* (Longman Paul, 1994) and his publications include *Unfinished Crossword* (Hazard Press, 1990).

Official Opening

When we were called to assemble
at the gates and the metal plaque
by the woman under the umbrella,
the rain was coming down in buckets,
& the man with the carved stick
made it plain and clear in his karakia
that the gods were extremely happy –

that the land was soaking it up;

years ago it was the only bush for miles
and that's always saddened me

they came up the Bridle Track and they saw it,
& you took out your notebook and you drew
a row of menacing mountains nothing like
the ones you knew at home
& God knows what was beyond – you didn't have a clue;

there was an unbelievably wide and flat land in front
stretching forever north and south in the heat,
and there were thickets, copses in the distance
against the low hills – one here, one there –

they were few and far between even then
& wouldn't take much milling.

Well that was then –
today's few words
are for planting young trees in a well-kept earth
with three freshwater springs nearby –

plenty to keep up the goodwill

here the roots would go back down the past –
a search for a time
when it was all tū kākāriki –
where the trees stood tall, & they stood green,
and they made you feel good

that's what I like about beginnings.

Time Past

some time ago I had a mate
who died near here –
a piece of wood came
flying out of a bandsaw;

below the mill, the river
flows almost dead still –
everything's dry as hell;

I remember we played
in a trench in your backyard
with WWI helmets
& a real machine gun
& a radio set;

when you died,
we took over two dozen eggs
to your mother –
she was sitting by the fire crying
& she said: "I wondered what I'd
have for dinner. . . ."

well, she's gone too –
& they buried her today,
I thought you should know that.

Karakia to a Silent Island

How do I greet you, motutapu?
How do I call across the darkness,
fish your still waters?

On what ears
do these words fall
& who is left to speak

for the tangatawhenua,
for the ghosts on the beach?

How do I greet you, motutapu?
How do I feel your pain,
your battlewounds?
Where man has fed on man,
how do I celebrate whanau?

As my canoe glides
through your silence –
only this –
kia ora ki a koe,
kia ora, kia ora, kia ora.

Anzac Day, Mount Fyffe, Kaikoura

All afternoon
as I climb this mountain
above the peninsula,
volleys of gunfire
have been coming up
from the rifle range below –

the percussion shakes the hills
& the sound rolls out
towards the ocean
where whales are cruising

in the silence between,
a bird calls,
& a cicada;

a mountain covered in snow
stands
in a deep blue sky

a warm wind bends the grass

in the valley
the river flows
like a ribbon of polished steel:

& in the hut logbook, this:
"To all the Kiwis who died
dreaming of mountains".

MICHAEL FANENE-BENTLEY

Michael Fanene-Bentley is a New Zealand-born Samoan of the aiga Fanene-Tui Samoa from the village of Saleilua, Falealili. He has an inherited interest in writing poems, short stories and novellas, reflecting the Samoan people's unique humour with underlying messages for his aiga and the people of Samoa. Michael has worked as a rehabilitation practitioner in the psychiatric field for the past 27 years, 20 of which were in Canada and among the native American First Nations' peoples.

Corned Beef by Candlelight

Tins of N.Z. corned beef from Hellaby's;
    gone to England
    to be auctioned at Sotheby's.
Fresh frozen mutton flaps;
    even boiled for a long time,
    chewy like licorice straps.
Frozen U.S. turkey tails,
    a luxury for me,
    like Americans eating quails.
Three minute noodles from Japan;
    they go far: one packet
    nearly feeds this man.
More pilchard tins from Chile;
    scatter over rice,
    but keep some back for Uele.
Those tins of mackerel today;
    no, for an occasion,
    to give as fa'alavelave.
Boiled cabbage and povi masima.
    rinse it well,
    too much salt's bad for tinā.

Open cans of pisupo lolo;
　　can't wait all year,
　　for our own palolo.
My meal imported by modernisation;
　　it's not all good for me, I know,
　　but will eat in moderation.
Taro, fruit, fish and banana
　　keep us healthy,
　　our food with mana.
Pass me the matches, by that pot handle,
　　I'm going outside to eat
　　my tinned corned beef by candle.

My sounds I do not hear

A Palagi, for an interview, to my village came.
Looking for sound.
Thinking: no I did not catch his name.
Do you hear the pounding of the surf upon your reef?
No I say,
Thinking: this sound must cause him much grief.
Do you hear the insects and birds in your bush?
No I say,
Thinking: maybe now I should give him the push.
Do you hear the roosters crowing by your fale in the morning?
No I say,
Thinking: now this is really getting boring.
Do you hear the wind blowing through your coconut trees?
No I say,
Thinking: nice shorts, glad I don't have those knobbly knees.
Do you hear the pigs rooting in that taro patch you planted?
No I say,
Thinking: I must have a problem, taking my sound for granted.
Do you not hear these sounds, or are you deaf, like that tree?
No I say,
Thinking: I hear them now, because he just told me.
Do you not hear any sounds when you are lying awake?
No I say,
Thinking: yes I must, but come one, give me a break.
Do you know I interview you, not to cause you any strife?
No I say,
Thinking: hang on, these are my sounds, I've heard them all my life.
Do you not hear these sounds because you're tired and need a break?

No I say,
Thinking: all my sounds must keep this Palagi awake.
Do you not listen to the sounds of your island, they are full of glory?
Yes I say,
Do you smell that smell?
No he say,
Thinking: I should tell him, well then, that's another story!

SIA FIGIEL

Sia Figiel is a single mother, poet, novelist, painter, teacher and journalist. She was born in Samoa and left when she was 16 for school in New Zealand. Acknowledged as the first woman novelist from Samoa, her first book *where we once belonged* (Pasifika Press) won the prestigious Commonwealth Writer's Best Book Award for the South East Asia–South Pacific region in 1997. She has published two other novels, a poetry collection and a CD recording of poetry with Teresia Teaiwa. She has been on extensive reading tours to New Zealand, Australia, Hawai'i, New York, Los Angeles and Europe, and was the first Pacific Islander to read at the Shakespeare Globe Theatre, London. She was the Distinguished Visiting Writer at the English Department of the University of Hawai'i at Manoa during Fall 2002. Sia is currently working on two novels; *After The Butterflies* and *The Love Monologues of the Masima Sisters*, to be published in 2003.

Between the steel bars

For the women (kailua correctional center)

Between the steel bars
You sit
In the dark
Of confinement
Solitary
A toilet at your feet
A shower at your feet
A mattress of steel at your feet
A holy bible too
At your feet

No sky
No tree
Not even the shadow of the Moon

And they've told me not to wear jewellery
And they've told me that I cannot see you
(A warning)
(So what if you've the same mother?)

After many conversations
And after many explanations
I walk towards you
(in the dark contemplating the silent corridor
the keys
the boots
so what if you've the same mother?)
and as I neared your cell
contemplating
(empty corridor)
you turned
and I see they've stuck your heart
to your eyes

because I saw it
beating
streaming too down
my face

(and you gave me your hands
and you gave me your hands
there
between the steel bars)

Songs of the fat brown woman

for sista grace (nichols) and the fat black woman

The fat brown woman move in the breeze
under the thatch of the small small fale
braiding sinnet
weaving stories
between the leaves of the pandanus

The fat brown woman sweat in the sun
lean on a coconut palm
swaying in the coconut sun
in colourful lavalava too small for her waist

The fat brown woman in the sea
is a sight to see
diving for blue fish red fish
an occasional eel
The fat brown woman walking home from the sea
is a sight to see

Around the fat brown woman there is
always a man or two
Big or small
Smiling smiling
At the way her hip sway
At the sound her thigh make
Around the fat brown woman there is
always a fly
or two
too

See the fat brown woman at a fa'alavelave
Directing the men the women
A fine mat here
A pig there
In her fat brown woman voice
in her fat brown woman style
gentle but firm
is the fat brown woman

When the fat brown woman hops on the bus the girls
and boys whisper
and men and women whisper
and children and cat whisper whisper
and pigs too sometimes
watch her sway
sway sway
and her arms moving like dat
and a shaking like dat
is her tummy too

they make room right behind the skinny
bus driver who gives her a big fat wink
the fat brown woman takes out a bright red
hanky wipes the sweat off her brow
pats her cheek
adjusts her dress/her bra/
her hip
chase away the flies
give the bus driver a mean look
Is going be a long way to market

So you can look all you want
And you can watch all you want
And you can stare all you want
But the fat brown woman will keep
swaying her hip
Keep swaying her hip
All the way to town

The fat brown woman watches miss universe on tee vee

What do you say is
going through the mind of the fat brown woman
watching miss universe the most beautiful woman in the world?
a aerobic instructa
wants to be a air hostess
a brain surgeon
perhaps
is her dream?
The fat brown woman add more coconut cream to the saka
and adjust her lavalava
call out to her big sista
e! we need to fix dat damn scale!

The fat brown woman's fat brown sista

Sits in the cool
of an air-conditioned room
directing an organisation
managing an institution
rewriting her constitution

Warning about the fat brown woman

The fat brown woman is quiet as you know
Doesn't say a word
An occasional laugh
She does not gossip
She does not lie
Will tell you straight away
Whether you sleeping with a fly
but piss the fat brown woman off and you see eyes
you never seen before
and a mouth you
never heard before
And if I was you I'd stay clear out of the way
Of the fat brown woman
When she's mad
When she's pissed
I'd stay clear out of the way
If I was you
I'd stay clear out of the way
Of whereva she going sit

A last note on the fat brown woman and shoes

No shoe fits the foot of the fat brown woman
No high heel
No low heel
No prince
No king
Can contain
Constrain
Confine the foot of the fat brown woman
Because the feet of the fat brown woman
Are grounded nicely to the bellies of
Her Mamas
The fat blue Pacific
The fat brown Earth
Thank you very much

TA'I GEORGE

Ta'i George writes: "My mother is from Pukapuka and my father from Atiu, in the Cook Islands. They were part of the wave of Polynesians who arrived in Auckland during the 1950s. It wasn't very long before they bought a house in the then brand new suburb of Otara and they live there still. So, I'm a 'South Auckland gal' born and bred. For the past sixteen years I've lived in Wellington."

My Mother's Coat

As a child
I felt protected and warm
Wrapped
in my mother's coat
It must have looked funny
Big brown eyes
Peering from its folds
As if that was all there was
to me

I remember
Its unique threads
Unusual and coarse
Their slenderness
belied their strength
Its tīvaevae-like panels
of thin fabric
An effective shield
against bitter winters
The colours loud
Shouting for attention
and space

My mother always wore
her coat with pride
Unfazed
by its highlighter effect
Marking her out

in a Papaā crowd
But blending beautifully
at every putuputuanga

I remember too
With youthful disdain
Discarding my mother's coat
Not for me
The uncool design
extravagant colouring
and awkward fit
I did not want
to be marked
If only
I knew then
What I know now

She wears it still
Her brooch of pride
brilliant and bright
And not long ago
I tried it on
after many years
Although it's not really me
It's because of her
I can sew
my own

Do Your People Tan?

"Do your people tan?"
I do a double take
"Are you talking to me?"
The direct stare replies
"Yes"
"What was the question again?"
"DOOO
YOOUUR
PEOPLE
TAANN?"
Classmates suppress giggles
"What kind of question is that?"

MAREWA GLOVER

Marewa Glover (Ngāti Hine, Ngāti Manu) was born in 1961 in Helensville. She went to 17 schools moving around Auckland, Coromandel and Australia, leaving with School Certificate to start work at age 16. She returned to university as a Mature Age Student, and in 2000 completed a doctorate in behavioural science at the Auckland School of Medicine. She won the award for Best Doctoral Thesis in 2001 and was awarded the Inaugural Maori Academic Excellence Award in Health Science in 2002. She started performing and publishing her poetry and short stories in 1986, and has since published in anthologies, journals, magazines and newsletters, mainly in Aotearoa, but also internationally. She has published two collections of poetry: *Mooncall* in 1990 and *Hui* in 2000.

Tangi

Going to tangi
is not some cute cultural practice
that we do
We're not going out of our way
to ensure the Maori process of grieving
is maintained, like we do
for our reo, our kapa haka
It's not a tourist attraction
or a lesson in cultural awareness
for us
We don't even go to ALL the funerals
of people we know
The seemingly "extended" leave
we take for close whanau & friends
is still frowned upon
It's not even that we maintain links
with "extended" whanau
We go to tangi
because people DIE
Maori people are dying
faster
earlier
more often!
Going to tangi

as *often* as we do
seems perfectly normal
to us.

No landmarks

tipuna have fallen
not as brave warriors in battle
on particular hillsides
they have not died
while halting the progress of the sun
in a particular sky
they have not sunk
into the stormy grasp of Tangaroa
out from a particular bay
no
they have decayed
from within
slowly erased
cell by cell
burned out
unheroic early deaths
smudging a printed whakapapa
the killer silent
unnoted

Hariru

"Tēnā koe" hongi kiss
"Kia ora" bump noses,
forehead while shaking hands
"Tēnā koe" pats on arm
kiss hongi kiss missed
that one oops glasses
clash "Sorry" "Tēnā koe e koro"
wrong hands mistake
each other left shakes
left "Kia ora!" Hug.
"Haven't seen you for
such a long time."
Tangi hug "Tēnā koe"

hongi or kiss? oops
that funny dance heads
like magnet ends
veer off causing
embarrassment, a laugh
"kia ora" "Hi" "Tena koe"
Breath, smells, face & hand oil
lipstick and tears shared
we chat and go for a cup of tea.

MICHAEL GREIG

Michael Greig was born in Nelson, New Zealand in 1953 and his heritage
includes Northern Cook Island, Scottish, English, Jewish and Portuguese
elements. He trained as a medical laboratory technologist and is still learning
new skills in many diverse trades. He is involved in things Pacific: its
ethnography, crafts, vaka and mythologies, as well as the proper use of vintage
sports cars. He has had work published in *Visions of the Pacific* (6th Festival of
Pacific Arts) and in Pacific Island newspapers, including the *Cook Island Press* and
the *Cook Island Star*, and is involved in performance poetry.

The Vocalisation

Kia angiangi te matangi
E fakarua no taua nii
Taku i tanu ra
Tera paa te Uru Aveatea
Te fakarihirihi i te maru o Araiara.

This warm breeze that swirls around and caresses,
makes the palms sway and dance,
hips moving.
Is it doing the same to the palms I planted far to the north?

Sitting in the evening, pen in hand, this same breeze tickles my skin, rekindles
memories and the need to return.
The velvet night is so bewitching

Himene Tuki

When I hear the Himene,
I see a bower of voices,
Sheltering, covering me.

The voice of my father,
A solo,
Lifting me with it.

We fly high above the present/past/future.

I heard him in Tukao, in Manihiki,
And in Rakahunga, amongst the choir.

We move through the historic past,
Advancing, looking back,
Moving into the future.

We are never alone.

Maui

Tera tana tautapa:

Toko miti, toko miti
Toko veta, toko veta.
Hi, hi, Maui,
Ha, ha, te henua,
Tu, tu, Maui.
Motu, motu Manihiki,
Motu, motu, Rakahanga.
Toko miti, toko miti,
Toku veta, toko veta.

Now it starts, this is his invocation.

Now look carefully, see this confused and tumbling sea,
In its midst there am I forcing the waves apart,
My muscles strain as the seas open up.
Here am I, see the land has arisen,
It is me standing tall on this new land.
There is Manihiki, to the north Rakahanga.
There, there, see the gap in the reef,
Remember the chant.

We remember, we remember,
We brought our home out of the sea,
We pulled it up from the deep.
We lived on it through all conditions.
Don't mess with us!

RORE HAPIPI

Born in 1935 in Oruanui, north of Taupo, Rore Hapipi has worked at numerous jobs (mainly manual) throughout New Zealand, though he is now retired and living in his home town. He has published poems, stories, articles and plays in numerous magazines and anthologies, including *Ta Ao Hou, Te Maori, Landfall, Mate, Arena, NZ Listener, Contemporary Maori Writing, Into the World of Light*, and *Te Ao Marama* (Vol. 1), dating back to the mid-1950s. He was awarded the Maori Affairs Writer's Award in 1975, won the Feltex Award for the best television script for 1981, and was the Katherine Mansfield Menton Fellow for 1984.

The Ballad of the Four Maori Boys

Three little Maori boys
    standing in a row
    all propped by Welfare
    man watch them go.

One's propped by Dole cheque
    the other P.E.P.
    the last's propped by Pension
    it's all theirs for free.

Three little Maori boys
    in boots and all
    props pulled out by Gov't
    Man watch them fall.

Fourth little Maori boy
    going it alone
    doing it his way
    burgling a home.

Good citizen sees Maori boy
    good citizen not impressed
    sends round a policeman
    Maori boy arrest.

Maori boy stands in Dock
    Stern Judge addresses
    ask Maori boy for reason
    Maori boy assesses.

Maori boy's excuse is
    at least he's off his arse
    so why don't they leave him
    instead they all harass.

Judge looks stern at Maori boy
    Maori boy looks stern at Judge
    six months for Maori boy
    now another one's on the bludge.

The 7th Day Adventist

On the 1st day I woke up with a frown
Then relaxed because the people were brown
Perhaps there were much they'd not understood
But at least they knew the land was good.

The 2nd day I woke up with a fright
To find that people were mostly white
I looked about for my coloured brothers
And found them mixed in with the others.

The 3rd day I woke, again with a fright
This time to see the land turned white
The goodness all sucked from out the soil
And shipped off as our country's spoil.

The 4th day I woke and cast about
For I thought I heard a horrible shout
It soon became too frighteningly clear
That the end of something was very near.

The 5th day I woke up with a scream
From thinking I'd had the awful dream
I lay there pondering the reason why
Then recalled I'd seen the rivers die.

The 6th day I woke to a terrible smell
And thought that I'd been cast in Hell
There was an awesome renting of the air
And smoke and fire was everywhere.

On the 7th day I woke and wished I'd not
For the air all round was filled with rot
The sun was obliterated from the sky
And not the sound of a solitary cry.

KU'UALOHA HO'OMANAWANUI

Ku'ualoha Ho'omanawanui is a Kanaka Maoli woman born near the sands of
One 'awa, Kailua, O'ahu, and raised in the mountainous Kaipuha'a region of
upper Wailua, Kaua'i. She spends most of her time as a student and part-time
lecturer at the University of Hawai'i at Mānoa. She is a founding editor of *'Ōiwi:
A Native Hawaiian Journal*, the first journal of its kind completely produced by
Kanaka Maoli which showcases Hawaiian writers and artists. When she is not
studying, dreaming or writing, Ku'ualoha likes to hang out with her husband
Ioane and their dog Ala'e.

laundry day sestina

We are so bored with this mechanical, thankless chore, the wash.
Zombie-like we move about methodically, serenely:
sort, lift, dump, pour, wait; lift, dump, sort, fold and wait
some more as the swishing thumping machines emit a steady hum.
I watch a man across the way slowly folding towels.
The air is heavy with the scent of soap.

Soap, ah soap! One of the most refreshingly clean smells, soap!
The only part I like when doing the wash
whether it's the car, the dishes, the dog, or just towels,
a pleasing smell to the nostrils which makes me dizzy, as I serenely
sit and wait and tap my feet against the drum. I start to hum
unbelievably silly ditties like Lambchop's "Never ending song" as I wait

and wait and wait
for this laundry to be done. I sigh. Watch the soap
breed bubbles that froth and sway back and forth. "A hum."
The woman behind me wants to do her wash.
I'm apologetic – she just looks at me serenely
as I move my things so she can load her towels.

She loads five machines with white towels.
Sometimes at the gym women line up and wait
for fluffy fresh white towels so serenely.
They will share these towels, but not their bottles of soap.
Bags of bottles – shampoos, conditioners, and soap with which they wash
their hair and shave their legs as they hum.

It is rush hour now. Outside the traffic starts to hum
as I wash and dry and fold my hand and bath and kitchen towels.
It's raining now – guess my car could use the wash.
While across the street a crowd of people wait
for the bus. I want to run outside and soap
up my hair and dance serenely

in the rain, like when I was young. But I just smile serenely
at the thought. Then sigh. And again I start to hum.
I pack up my laundry, put away the soap
set it securely in the basket, an anchor atop the towels.
I make my way outside through those who still watch and wait,
fellow pilgrims at the altar of the wash.

The watercolour sunset sky is gold and pink against a grey wash
and as the sun slants through the drizzle, I wait
but no rainbow comes. I head home, hair covered with a towel.

The Horseshoer

Working hands his: large, rough, strong, scarred, capable hands,
knuckles nicked by barbed wire and barroom brawls,
short nails stubbed square defy cleanliness,
remnants of earth and grease ever present.

They can fine tune the reluctant engine of a forklift or semi,
they can "persuade" a recalcitrant horse or lover; mostly they are hard, these hands
wrapped around steel – steering wheel or beer can,
always curled into a tight protective fist.

Steel grey gunmetal skies loom dark and distant
as gods sing prayers, stir an amber sea with their breath
An ocean lonely and distant, easily crossed in your wa'a of choice;
the expert navigator will not drown in Wākea's realm.

After all these years, memory still treads on unspoken words,
stilled breath, intermingled, an amorphous cloud:
why there, why then, why that, why her – what now?

Curled around the engine of a Ford 250, grease smudged with sweat on your brow,
back bent under the hood, you grin that boyish grin, the one that softens your cool green eyes,
extend one calloused hand out, palm up
as you explain that horseshoeing school pays the bills and I should be happy
her job keeps her away long enough for me to pass you another beer.

KERI HULME

Poet, short story writer, novelist and fisher, Keri Hulme was born in Otautahi, New
Zealand, in 1947. She has Scots, English and Maori ancestry; her tribal affiliation is
to Kāi Tahu (Kāti Rakiamoa, Kāi Te Ruahikihiki). Writing fulltime since 1983,
Hulme gained international recognition with the novel *the bone people* (which won
the New Zealand Book Award for Fiction, the Mobil Pegasus prize for Maori
writing, both in 1984, and the Booker-McConnell award in 1985). Keri's main
interests are her whanau, friends, reading, painting, food and fishing, especially
whitebaiting (the reason why she continues to live in an isolated area on the west
coast of the South Island, New Zealand).

Hōkioi

"Have you ever been windwhipped?
Had your belly kneaded by want?
So it is with me, friend,
so it is with me.

I am given lone islands
with deep kilts of kelp,
stray birds and tired ghosts
to shelter in my arms –
I am a slender skein of muscle and bone
to stand against fear on their behalf.

I smell bad times coming,
a sharp intake of death,
I am eating our way to safety
building fat rib walls against famine
saving that monthly flush of blood
for real wounds
collecting anyone else's breath
against
the rending
the ravening
the hellbent raving cry of war.

> *The wind is rising, e hoa –*
> *may all the nightfliers be friendly"*

Silence
. . . on another marae

E ngā iwi o ngāi tahu
(for Rowley Habib, who asked the question)

Where are your bones?

My bones lie in the sea

Where are your bones?

They lie in forgotten lands
stolen, ploughed, and sealed

Where are your bones?

On southern islands
sawed by discovering winds

Where are your bones?

Whisper:
Moeraki: Pūrakaunui: Arahura:
Okārito: Murihiku: Rakiura . . .

Where are your bones?

Lying heavy on my heart

Where are your bones?

Dancing as songs and old words in my head
deep in the timelessness of mind

Where are your bones?

Here in my gut
strong in my legs walking
knotting my fists
but

Where are your bones?

Auē!
My bones are flour,
ground to make an alien bread . . .

Mihi. Greeting. Weeping hello.
And to me, standing out as though
I'm the cripple in a company of runners;
to me, pale and bluegrey-eyed,
skin like a ghost, eyes like stones;
to me, always the manuhiri when away from home –
the weeping rings louder than the greeting.

First sleep in Te Rangiita

Even after the welcoming, the hongi line, and the kai, I can still feel uneasy. Other people, other tribes, are here, and they carry their own burdens. And I can never know all these islands intimately . . . the land is strange, the people strangers, and myself the bird of passage journeyed away from home.

Alone in a sea of breathing
with a hook dream
waiting in the dark

The wind bangs the door like a stranger
and the rain clatters
clawfooted on the roof

Auē! Moeraki, Okārito –
my searock people
are miles fogged with distance
long silences away . . .

Winesong 23

There is a name I use in the daytime
and a name I use at night
names for walking on the left side
names for trampling down the right.

                Pass the bottle, lady.

I have a name I use at the tideline
and another for swimming in the sea
and one for when I'm landbound
and several for flying free.

                Pass the bottle, lady,
                observe the level of the wine.

I have a name I am called in my living
and a secret one waiting for death
a name for the time I am breathing
and a last name for the last breath.

Pass the bottle, lady,
observe the level of the wine –
time flows slowly, lady.

Names from friends and lovers
names from enemies
names in war and fighting
and names in peace:
I have one name here before me
another to leave behind,
and not one name fits all me
not any name in time –

Pass the bottle, lady,
observe the level of the wine;
time flows slowly, lady –
all down the line

and what name would you give me?

Winesong 15

I will sing a lovesong
– do not hide your ears
it is time for heartsongs and it is time for tears –
lady, I am a lover
lady, I am a thief
and I need your heart, love
as I need wine and tide and beach –

I will sing a tidesong
to while away your fears
you will hear the sea sound, you will hear deep prayers
but lady, I am a loner
and truly, I am a thief
and I will keep your heart-love
within my bottle's reach

and take it out in moonlight
and finger it with awe
until mazed with night caresses
I'll praise the bottle more.

When I sing this winesong
you'd better stop your ears
it only brings you emptiness
and strange and hopeless cares –

Lullaby for a Stone Doll

O I could suck on their brains!
Those long-tongued spiteful men!

Their lewd words
rob me of my place
I am footloose on a barren way
searching for something lost
never mind! I shall be all parents to you –
here, a plaited cover, a cloak to keep you from the cold
like any other winterborn child,
muka to protect that raw navel and titoki oil
and I shape you, with caress, as any massaging mother does her soft newborn
hah! but that will teach them to jeer
Hine-i-tūrama my highborn self –

I'll charge you with so much love
that you'll laugh
and cry real tears
and I will hear your heartbeat
ticking away like a small cicada
at night.

And I even have a name for you, son –
Tūwairua
– do you like it?
We shall be able to say our names together
when we go down to the dark,
you and I.

They say I am mad
I am made I am mad but
I dwell secure on earth
under any sky
and care for all I have wrought –
whatever you are, baby,
you are safe with me –

what am I afraid of?
Not that mixture of fist and tongue they thrust out
but of hurting without comfort without surcease
even after the dark
forgetting to care being hopeless
the eel to get my heartmeat is despair

but still I hold you
with love –

O I could eat them!

WITI IHIMAERA

Witi Ihimaera was born in Gisborne, New Zealand. He is a prizewinning
novelist, short story writer, librettist, playwright and editor of numerous books.
He is also Associate Professor of English at the University of Auckland, and a
respected commentator on Maori and Pacific literature, art, film, education,
culture and politics. Witi is one of only two New Zealand writers to have won the
Wattie (now called the Montana) New Zealand Book of the Year Award three
times: with his first novel, *Tangi* in 1973, with *The Matriarch* in 1986 and *Bulibasha,
King of the Gypsies* in 1994.

L'Ultimo Giorni

(Traversing the Underground, London, 24 June 1998)

In these Last Days entry is automated
and Charon has been made redundant
No gatekeeper waits at the entrance
(the gold coin in the mouth has been replaced
by Travelcard with passport-sized photograph)

*In the future Mastercard, American Express
or Diners Card may be accepted*

The descent is made by escalator
rumbling, vertiginous, swift and gleaming
(the ferry is now obsolescent and the River Styx
was drained of its dark waters many years ago)
You are delivered from the Overworld
to the fetid humid darkness below

Stand on the right beware of pickpockets
keep your belongings with you at all times

You enter a labyrinth offering choice of destination
Oxford Circus, Charing Cross, Waterloo Station
The worm holes are plastered with billboards
advertising the riches of Inferno
(the glittering realm of the Underworld is seductive
better to rule in Hell than to serve in Heaven)

The next train terminates at Elephant & Castle
surveillance cameras are in constant operation

Make your choice, go swiftly to the platform
of your desire for, see, the dark train comes
(Bakerloo, Victoria, Jubilee, Hounslow & Piccadilly
are the suburbs of this wicked City of Dis)
The doors are opening, your destiny/destination
awaits but –

    Oh, step backward angel, and return
    to the Overworld while you can

    Stand clear of the doors mind the gap
    mind the gap mind the gap mind the
    gap

Oh Numi Tutelar

(At the British Museum, London, 25 June 1998)

    3 in the morning
The streets deserted   I had forgotten
only derelicts & prostitutes are abroad in the night
forsaken lovers locked out
    (and Maori attending dawn ceremonies)

Make way, Britannia, Albion, Victoria Imperatrix,
make way our putatara are braying to bring down
your walls   The dawn is coming and with it
Magi, gift bearers from the South

Piki mai, kake mai, homai te wai ora
ki ahau

We have come
from the utmost ends of the earth   a tribe of travellers
with our own Queen, ministers & warrior escort
to the land of our Treaty partner where
our treasures have been plundered
    (and Roma & I halfway round the world
    to read in a stairwell)

Make way, O Egypt, ancient Assyria, Greece, Rome
make way   our own Cleopatra comes amid you
Semiramis, Te Arikinui, Imperatrix of Aotearoa
Maori women, gift bearers from the South

Haramai te toki, hui e, haumi e, taiki e

So here we are
climbing upward   the Museum opening unwilling
to the dawn, the kai karanga calling, the warriors
pulling us in & Maramena asks, "How can our
culture so small survive in this treasure house
of many cultures?"
    (The answer is simple: Godzilla was wrong
    size does not matter)

Oh antiquities of Asia, make way, lions of Judah
bow down, Babylon, stela of Islam make way
give space, Oh Nimrod, Horus, Mahomet
we are iwi Maori, gift bearers from the South

E taonga tū mai, tū mai, tū mai

And in the great hall
for the first time we see   the past before us
the treasures of our ancestors a Pharaonic ransom
of immense psychic power, indeed we live
with our past   the ghosts among us
    (How can I explain? We have always walked
    backwards into our future)

Oh, ancestors, stand forever! Stand for yesterday!
Stand for today! Stand for tomorrow! Stand
for always! Stand! Stand! Stand!

Take heed, O Gods of all other worlds, numi tutelar
We come chanting, we come singing, we come
proudly from Rangiātea, there our seed was sown
We come, still voyaging by star canoes
by aurora australis

We are from savage islands, far to the south
we move through your constellations
make way   and where there is one
oh Gods, there are a thousand

We are Magi, bearing gifts
and our dawn is coming

   Ka Ao, ka Ao, ka awatea

Un Semplice Storia

(Leaving London, 7 July 1998)

If I should die in a foreign land
    do not leave me there
place me upon the bright strand of sky & sea
    set my eyes southward
and, just as the sun goes down
    call Hine Te Ariki
    to come for me

MONICA KAIWI

Monica A. Ka'imipono Kaiwi is a secondary-school English teacher at the
Kamehameha Schools in Honolulu, Hawai'i, where she teaches Hawaiian, Pacific
and American literature. She is currently a doctoral student in the English
department at the University of Auckland, New Zealand.

"Hey, haole lady . . ."

I

Hey, haole lady with your token Hawaiian in a head lock
        what do you mean,
            "being Hawaiian is the color of your heart"?

Do you feel the tug,
        push and pull of your kupuna through your na'au?
Are you driven
        by a sense of obligation
        and responsibility to your people?
Do you rage
        and ache at the pain
        of the 'āina and nā 'ōiwi?

        being Hawaiian is not skin or heart
        It is iwi and 'uhane
            connecting me to my kupuna,
            my mo'okū'auhau,
            my heritage given by birth . . .
                not for sale to anyone.

II

Hey, haole lady who wants to be Hawaiian
      what do you mean I need
      to "do" my incantations
      to "pray" to the shark god
       to protect us from all the man-eating sharks in the Kaiwi Channel
      to put lākī in my bathing suit in order to win the race?

Keep your foolish superstitions to yourself
      and don't blame
      your ignorance
             on my ancestors.

IMAIKALANI KALAHELE

Artist, poet and political activist, Imaikalani Kalahele was born in Hawai'i in 1950. He is a graduate of McKinley University and currently lives in Kalihi on the island of O'ahu.

Ode to Fort Street

when pigs walked
from the harbor
to the ice house

Kalakaua played
at Alekoki
and Hawaiians
ruled their
homelands

now

where pigs walk
marble and McDonald's
obscure the harbor

Kalakaua stands
frozen in bronze
and the missionary
sons are still
inventing history

pigs, pigs, pigs

once they walked
on cloven hooves
up dirt paths

now

they walk
on sidewalks
and
wear Italian shoes

Before had England

Before had England
Even before had
Jesus!
there was a voice
and the voice was

maoli.

Make a fist

Make a fist
hold it high

Hear the
pahu scream.

Make a fist
hold it high

Let our ancestor's
rage infest your
intentions.

Make a fist
hold it high.

Plant the resistance
deep.

Kanu! Kanu!
Kanu now.
Ho'oulu hou.
Ho'oulu hou.
Ho'oulu hou.

Huli.

O'ahu

into the valley
Lua's water falls
deep
feeding a young
island
born
was Ka'ala draped
in clouds
born
were the Ko'olau
long and majestic

hānau
O'ahu
child of Papa
and
Lua
Ē Papa ē
Ē Lua ē
Ē O'ahu
ē

Hui 'Imi Pākīpika

tec – tec – tec
deep in the 'awa
we heard a call

tec – tec – tec
asking to come
and share

tec – tec – tec
from Waikīkī, Makiki
and Kapālama

we come to prepare
our journey
to go

At the shore we gathered
resting in the shade
of a hau tree.

Then,

shedding our skins
for fins
we slide into the water
to begin our journey
Hui 'Imi Pākīpika.

Rise up

Rise up.
From the roots
to the Gods.
Rise up
pass the history
and share the mana'o.
Rise up.
Rise up.
Out of the
ashes of colonial
thinking.
Rise up.
Rise up.
Rise up.
Pass the mana.
Drink the 'awa.
Pai! Pai!
Drink the 'awa.
Rise up
and hold high our
spears.
Rise up.
Rise up.
Rise up.
E ala! Kū'ē!

E Hānai 'Awa a Ikaika ka Makani

Returning once more
over the mo'os back

Brothers of an
ancient family

gathered.

From the northeast
below Maui's hook

to the Southern Cross
and the lands below

a meeting of
mana was set.

We came with verse
in hand and found

the 'awa was
still there.

MĀHEALANI KAMAUU

Born in January 1947 in the Lawai, Kaua'i, Hawai'i, Māhealani Kamauu is the
Executive Director of the Native Hawaiian Legal Corporation. She received the
Elliott Cades Award for Literature in 1993 and her poems have been included in
numerous publications, including *Sister Stew* (Bamboo Ridge Press, 1985),
Literary Arts Hawai'i (No. 91, New Year 1989), *Na Mamo* (Hartwell, 1996), *O'ahu
Review* (Balaz, 1997), *Manoa, a Pacific Journal of International Writing* (1998) and
volumes 1 and 2 of *'Oiwi: A Native Hawaiian Journal*, published in 1998 and 2002.

Calvary at 'Anaeho'omalu

In a hotel lobby
Near 'Anaeho'omalu Bay
A resort manager's grand idea
Of Christmas in Hawai'i –

A two-story Norfolk
Festooned with implements
Of Hawaiian dance:
Feather gourds, 'ulī'ulī,
Gaily colored and fastened
With braided hau;

Double gourds, ipu heke,
Suspended by intricate netting;
Split bamboo, pū'ili,
Backdrop of kapa –
All gifts from an
Ancient intelligence,
The whole show
Razzle dazzle electric,
Undulating, haole hula,
to soft offshore breezes.

I stand at Christ's tree,
And from another temple
Illumined by oils of kukui hele pō
And the moon goddess Hina,
An intoxication of holy communion:
From a stranger's silver chalice pours
The dark blood of ancestors.

Pulsating
Blood and sinew
Sensate with the drumming of pahu,
Clash of kā lā'au,
Rattle of kūpe'e,
Rapping of ipu heke;
Voices rise out of shadows
And intone an ancient cadence:

Ē Laka ē   (Oh Laka
Pūpū weuweu   Oh wild wood bouquet
E Laka e   Oh Laka
'Ano'ai aloha ē   Greetings and salutations
'Ano'ai aloha ē   Greetings and salutations
'Ano'ai aloha ē   Greetings and salutations)

In a hotel lobby
'Anaeho'omalu spinning,
I feel tethered and hammered through,
Wild among dark branches
Snared by voices on angry winds.

Host Culture (Guava Juice on a Tray)

"Host culture."
What euphemistic bullshit –
Pure, unadulterated H.V.B.
They act like
They was invited –
Like all these years,
We been partying
Or something;
It's like
Getting fucked in the ass
Is supposed to be
A turn on –
Get real!
Whoever thought up
That crap
Deserves to get whacked
Let's get one thing straight:
Nobody invited anybody –
They pulled a number on us,
Big time!
It's the same old, same old –
They move in
And before you know it
They take over:
The guys in the house
End up on the streets;
The guys with scratch
End up sucking wind;
The warriors,
They all in the joint;
The wahines
They all strung out;
The kids,
They getting hauled off
By C.P.S. –
The old folks
No can handle –
Nobody like listen to them anymore;
The "leftovers",
They all "psycho out",
Or in the churches
Thinking they fucked up.

How you gonna act
When you think about
The haole teacher
Giving your mother
A hard one across the face
For talking Hawaiian;
Or the Queen
Tripping out in prison;
Or the old gods
On display
In New England parlors
Their balls cut off –
You know, they still trying
To castrate us
You hate to think like that
But seem like
They keep trying
To convince you that
Getting raped
Is very maika'i
We supposed to
Catch our thrills
Because one stealth bomber
Named *Spirit of Aloha* –
Or because hula sell
Like Amway in Japan?
Every friggin' ripoff
Get one nice Hawaiian tag –
Like we all right with it
Like we gave permission or something
Too much, these guys –
We stay all bust,
All coma out,
And they act like everything way cool
That's probably why
N.W.A.
Get nothing over the bruddahs
They doing crack
Smoking the crystal meth
They poking heroin
They pounding wahines
They kicking ass big time!
They way beyond
That red rag bullshit

They carrying pieces
They taking guys out
They fucking nuts!
The way they feel
You can kiss their ass.

Uluhaimalama

*Written in honor of Queen Lili'uokalani on the hundredth
anniversary of her birthday. The Queen named her garden
Uluhaimalama. The kaona, or meaning, of that name is this: as
plants grow up out of the dark into the light, so shall light come to
the Hawaiian nation. Feasting on stones is a reference to "Kaulana
Nā Pua", the song of protest written after the overthrow of the
Hawaiian nation in 1893. The song says that Hawaiians would
rather eat stones than accept any annexationist proffer from the
United States. (1 September 1993)*

We have gathered
With manacled hands;
We have gathered
With shackled feet;
We have gathered
In the dust of forget
Seeking the vein
Which will not collapse.
We have bolted
The gunner's fence,
Given sacrament
On bloodstained walls.
We have linked souls
End to end
Against the razor's slice.
We have kissed brothers
In frigid cells,
Pressing our mouths
Against their ice-hard pain.
We have feasted well
On the stones of this land:
We have gathered
In dark places
And put down roots.

We have covered the Earth,
Bold flowers for her crown.
We have climbed
The high wire of treason –
We will not fall.

*

(O Moon, lift the brittle white dust,
The red augury of tears;
Call forth the sea,
Enchant its blue heart;
Form this place holy,
And holy again.)

What My Mother Said to Me

Come here!
I said, come here!
Where the hell you been?
Where the fuck you think you was going?
You on dope or something?
No lie to me.
More betta you tell your friends support you.
Quit school already – you only wasting everybody's time.
At the rate you going, more betta you get out.
Don't gimme that.
What kind report card is this?
That's what they teach you at school?
As all you can think about, is hanging around the beach?
I not going to no more school conferences.
I not wasting my time talking to teachers.
You tell the principal I said go to hell.
They kick you out, that's your tough luck.
No come crying to me.
You lucky you even get chance for go school –
I had to work – I *wish* I was you.

No come in here asking for money.
No think you going drive the car.
You wen take my cigarettes?
You wen take money from my wallet?

What I told you about taking money from my wallet?
No make me laugh – you going pay me back,
You going get one job.
What kind job you think you could get?
The rate you going, you going land in O.P.

By the way, how your friends got that car?
Where they got that Bug, anyway?
You know anything about that fire down the school?
You had something to do with that haole girl down the beach?
Answer me!
No think jus cause you get hair growing up your ass you too big for get licking.
Come here so I can punch your face.
No look at me like that.
Whassa matter? You cannot talk?

Bereaved Daughter-in-law

We die soon enough –
Brides reunited in Christ,
Men gone to ether, flame,
Or vaulted in, whatever.
In that final agony
Heroin and a good beer
Might do for some;
For others,
A contemplation of the Divine,
I don't know.
My husband once told me
About coming upon
Young lovers on a hill
At twilight
Beside Kewalo's surf
After bringing the nets in;
I guess the dusky hill,
The surf's languor,
The innocents,
Long black hair down
Her slender back, astride,
Caught him by surprise.
He left quickly

Unnoticed and embarrassed;
He told me about it
When words
Were awkward
Between us. I blushed
Feeling he somehow imagined us there.
Yesterday mom died.
Her soul was routed through
The Mormon tabernacle
By Times Supermarket.
She once scolded me
For my irreverent poems,
And raged when
I turned her son in
For his demons.
"What kind of Hawaiian are you!"
Her recriminations stung
But yesterday
I kissed her face and
Caressed her hands;
For love of her
Queues formed at the coffin
Out the great hall, around the corner,
Down the city block –
So many tears,
And mine the least among them,
Feeling unworthy to approach even
Kapu moe,
Prostrate;
Yet she would always have me
Take my place
As family.
Mom, please accept our gifts,
Your son's carved palaoa, my leis,
Forgive us,
Help us work out our love
And I know you understand now
I can't help
The poems.

KAURAKA KAURAKA

Kauraka Kauraka was born in Rarotonga in 1951, and educated in the Cook Islands, New Zealand, Fiji, Papua New Guinea and Hawai'i. He published six collections of poetry in English and Cook Islands Maori, including *Return to Havaiki* (1985), *Dreams of a Rainbow* (1987) and *Manakonako, Reflections* (1992). As well as being a writer, a musician and photographer, he was by profession an anthropologist with the Ministry of Cultural Development, Cook Islands. Kauraka Kauraka passed away in 1997.

Rainbow Woman

You appear to me in dreams day and night
Your gold and black hair flows
Forming hills and valleys in full colour
Causing the living dead to look up

You came to me in bone and blood
The marrow still white the water flows
Creating coconut trees and pandanus groves
Leaving sweet fragrance of your hands in the wind

You penetrate my eyes with tender rays
Your brilliance doubling my vision
Illuminating the lava sealed paths in my soul
Releasing the fire and water within

You offer me omens of Po
Gifts of earth nail and hair
Of maire tuitui and ginger stone
Your rainbow from your seven heavens

Moko

Moko went into the forest beyond his home
spotted the right place to perform
and sing his father's song:
   "Moko mai, neke mai,
   Meke mai, ne!"
This was his lure for a mate
with eggs in mind
From behind a fern she came dancing
then followed him under a stone
to dance some more.

Rainbow Priest

Guardian of white light
that makes golden rainbows
You chant to the gods
for special berries
to paint the colours
of the rainbow
Difficult to capture
your face burns
like the desert sun
Yet you can be trusted
to create colour and wonder
Tonight you will meet
your brother from Havaiki-Po
the guardian of black light
that makes silver rainbows
He chants to the gods
for special rains
to change the colours
of your rainbow
His face is easy to recognise
because it shines
like the shadow of the first moon

PHIL KAWANA

Phil Kawana was born in Hawera, Aotearoa/New Zealand in 1965. He is of Ngaruahinerangi, Ngāti Ruanui, Ngāti Kahungunu ki Wairarapa and Rangitāne descent, and his whakapapa also includes Scots and English. Phil is known primarily as a short story writer, having twice won the Huia Short Story Award, and through his critically acclaimed collection *Dead Jazz Guys* (Huia, 1996). He has been widely anthologised, broadcast and studied, and has performed both his poetry and prose at festivals, libraries and schools throughout Aotearoa. He currently lives in Wellington.

Breeder Boy

Pony-tailed Breeder Boy
with leather jacket
& caffeine-studded eyes,

buzzing off Cafe Girls,
with their funky clothes
and done-that shoes.

He's window-shopping
to pass the day,
his life lent shape

by glimpses of dreams,
by a face with Hope,
by a meeting with angels.

Breeder Boy unties his hair
and becomes Tribal Herbsman.
There are pinprick burns on his shirt.

And the sun is shining
somewhere beyond this Misty Morning
that is half-Marley, half-Monet, and is passing

slowly into afternoon, easing
into the day like his hands
along the thighs of a beautiful woman

late one night in Lyall Bay.
The soft clouds taste the sky
with candyfloss tongues,

and Breeder Boy smiles knowingly,
slips his fingers into the earth,
and lifts his face to the sun.

Dogs & Dinghies

Down here now, it's just
    dogs and dinghies.
All the rangatahi have moved
into the city, all
except for the Johnston boy
who's a little simple.
The dogs are all old and tired.
The dinghies are upturned
above the tideline,
prows to the hills.
There's the old people, of course,
slipping between the past
and the time before that,
the time when the setting sun
sparkled in someone's eyes,
threw silhouettes upon the sea.

The Instant of a Smile

Within the instant of a smile
I have known you,
have tasted your sweat-salted skin,
teased your nipple with the tip of my tongue,
traced your hips with the palm of my hand.

Within the instant of a smile
I have taken your slender fingers,
held them to my face, my chest,
let fingernails circle, tattoo my back,
let your thighs enfold me,
tight and warm and yielding.

Within the instant of a smile
I have known these things
and realising I shall know no more,
I have smiled back
and walked away.

Untitled (#79)

Somebody should tell those
young people
there is no such thing as
        racial discrimination
in our country – they have as much chance in life as any *ordinary* person.
Somebody should show them
    that we are not prejudiced against
                    them –
if only we could keep them
            out of gangs
and off glue-bag streets.
Time was when you could give them
        a pub and a guitar
and they'd be happy, the way they
    were meant to be
        but now
they've had their heads filled
with all this radical mumbo-jumbo
and they're marching about trying
    to steal land they say is theirs!
I just don't know what the world is coming to.
I mean, really!
How can you legalise theft?

Hongoeka Bay

I am very drunk,
a sight you should remember well
but I am trying not to remember

When the vodka is gone
I shall take your letters from my pocket
roll them into a candle in the bottle

watch the flames kiss your name,
the ash tumble inwards, then
I shall lie back on the cold sand

and wait for the tide
and the stingrays to drag this pain
far out to sea.

NINA KIRIFI-ALAI

Nina was born in Iva, Savai'i, Samoa and grew up in Apia. She migrated to New Zealand in 1985 and went back to Samoa in 1991. She found that all her friends were in good jobs, some with degrees. Realising the value of education she enrolled in the New Start programme in late 1993. She has never looked back since. She received her BA in 1997, majoring in Women's Studies, and is the first Pacific Island Women's Studies graduate. She has also completed an LLB from the University of Auckland.

Virginity

sorry mate
it's gone
YOU disappointed!?
Me own body
me do
me want
me boss.

Who?
You persisted
you can't stomach
the thought of one of your brothers
beating you to it.

You boys
better get your act together
we're not bones
for you dogs to compete for.

HINEWIRANGI KOHU

Hinewirangi Kohu was born in 1947 with tribal affiliations to Ngāti Kahungunu and Ngāti Ranginui. She is well-known as a multi-media artist, having exhibited at locations throughout New Zealand. She is also a political activist, and has served as the New Zealand board member of the International Indian Treaty Council and a representative for the Nuclear Free and Independent Pacific movement. Hinewirangi is a teacher, conducting workshops on all aspects of the Maori philosophies of mental, physical, and spiritual well-being, with expertise in traditional Maori parenting and healing; Maori flute-making; and indigenous poetry and drama. She has published two collections of poetry, *Screaming Moko* (Tauranga Moana Press, 1986) and *Kanohi ki te Kanohi* (Moana Press, 1990).

Sisters

Tonight sisters
    I hear your pain
        feeling it calling
calling, calling
    across the crested wave
Te Moana nui a Kiwa
    it's an old pain
long   many moons
        old
Here
    on the shores
of the Great Turtle
    I ponder your calls
it is a tangi
    a karanga
        a waiata
that calls me
    to return
to our land
    our whenua
        our mother earth

to our dreams
      our moemoeā
           our spirit walk times
they
      say you are not worthy
      our own say so
           I have walked that pain
      I know
it is of our sisters
           not yet part
of the sacred circle
it stabs, cuts, slices
at our breasts
      our core
           our centres
                our ngākau
spirit wings fly
      protection
           soaring to untouchable
heights   crests   maunga
I was at that edge
      not sure
           ending
              jumping
or
      staying
           blanking
              not owning
but
      memories
           they don't die
they live
      in me
           inside
              deep
twisting rocks
      I survived
           not victim
riding the winged one
      I will return
still remembering
      hurt
           pain
love

```
                    remembering
the silent prayers
                    karakia
wise one
            who knew my role
my mothering
            my nuturing
processing of healing
            gentle returning
remembering
            when my head bows
it will be to Mauao
            Moumoukai
                    Pirongia
feet
            planted
                    firmly
on her
            my heart in my hands
Your
            hands
                    his hands
moulding
            woman's work
                    rituals
helping
            āwhina
                    healing
                            you
May we meet
            Kanohi ki te kanohi
face to face
                    ihu ki te ihu
breath to breath
            Tihei Mauri ora.
```

Wise one, Old one

```
In the tipi
            by the night fire
you came
            with sage
```

sacred cedar beads
                    cedar offerings
to the fire
          offerings to the wise ones
your story
          there was an original mother
a wise one, old one
          she saw in her children
                    invaders
                              killers/murderers
                    rapists
          abusers
she decided to send them to the
                    four corners
                    four winds

to some she gave
          white corn
                    go where the white butterflies
                              fly
where the white beans
          grow
                    there build your homes

to some she gave
          the yellow corn
                    go where the yellow butterflies
                              fly
where the yellow beans
          grow
                    there build your homes

to some she gave
          the black corn
                    go where the black butterflies
                              fly
where the black beans
          grow
                    there build your homes

to some she gave
          red/copper corn
                    go where the red/copper butterflies
                              fly
where the red/copper beans

grow
there build your homes

to each she gave
one portion of the knowledge of life
one portion of the knowledge of healing

there will come a time
when you have recognised
the invader in you
the invader around you
you will return
to the sacred circle
you will know
the wise ones, old ones
you will lay your
sacred bundles
at each other's feet
I lay my bundle at your feet
Hinewirangi
as I have taken your
sacred bundles

KAPULANI LANDGRAF

Born and raised in Pūʻahuʻula, Kāneʻohe, Kapulani Landgraf is a Hawaiian
photographer. She received her BA in Anthropology from the University of
Hawaiʻi at Mānoa and her MFA in Photography from Vermont College. In 1995
Kapulani's book *Nā Wahi Pana o Koʻolau Poko* was the winner of Ka Palapala
Poʻokela Award for Excellence in Illustrative Books.

. . . devastation upon devastation . . .

The land is unstable,
having no root for sustenance.
Overthrown are the loʻi of Luluku
by the iron boar.

The iron fish have stripped the land,
exposing the entrails of Papa.
Naked in the hala of Ho'oleina'iwa,
fallen is the ripe fruit of Kekele.
Digging, turning over, delving into the past.

Broken is the kapu of Kumukumu,
resounding is the heiau drum of Kāne.
Punalu'u's kukui, its rooted veins, are distressed;
the gushing tears of Hi'ilaniwai cease falling.
Tortured with grief is Kahoe,
torrents pouring on the broken coral of Lo'e.
Excruciating is the pain of the ancestors,
loud is the weeping and wailing.
Digging, turning over, exposing the past.

Resonant, thunderous, clamoring proclamation;
'Āinakea is breathless in the dark clouds.
The whirlwinds twist beneath the earth,
gushing forth are the springs in the road.
The great waters of the upland rage;
the highway is filled with fleeing pariahs.
The ash rain of Ha'ikū endlessly pelting,
sinister upheaval consuming the land.
Digging, turning over, revealing the past.

The gods return, multitudinous, to dwell in the cliffs;
in the rains of Ko'olau, the spirits gather,
grieving everywhere, remorseful throughout.
Echoing through the mountains,
it comes, it rises, it moves on, it broadens, it extends forth.
Lofty are the inaccessible cliffs of Ko'olau,
rising high, in the slaughter.
Ceaseless is the devastation of the island.
Digging, turning over, seeking the past.

MARAMA LAURENSON

Marama Laurenson, born 1950, has tribal affiliations with Tuhourangi, Tuwharetoa, Te Atihaunui-a-Paparangi, Ngāti Kahungunu ki Wairarapa, Kati Huirapa o Ngai Tahu. She has worked as a history researcher, a senior policy analyst, and as a report and policy writer for the public and private sectors as well as being a tutor for literacy and numeracy in both the prisons and the community. She maintains an interest in the claimant process, presently participating in a claims committee in the Wairarapa.

Tahu Brown Parata – Ol' rolly eyes

I remember you, ol' rolly eyes
One flipped up, the other down
In a tall still frame of man

Your kids left the toast plate empty
With practised speed
Under my useless hand
I looked at you, ol' rolly eyes
. . . one flipped up, the other down

On a grey Puke morning
Mavis in petticoat got up weary
You in a singlet splashed your face
At the wash-house concrete tub
Wiry hair jerked
As you turned, said, what!
Ol' rolly eyes, one up, the other down

A winter Roxburgh day
Raisins a treat in meat paste jar
Sent to a room without adults
We heard the rumble of talk and laughter
And pictured ol' rolly eyes
One up and one down

Otematata, summer bleached
Euclid monsters hauling the dirt
You drove into piles and dumped again

Each day home
To Lindsay's gasps and waving hands
Through cot rails
At your first footstep

Otago heat
Ripening apricots not to be eaten
Except as bottled treasure
Put there by women
As you pitted and sliced

Patsy bulging with Tapi's child
Brought hankies for my birthday
Ian a shilling pared from a half-moon wallet
David two china ducks
. . . things to look at in the car, and fiddle with
As the sight of your rolly eyes
Lolled in my mind remembering, family

Later you shared the veil
Of battle and bash on the other side of the world
Your mates said you rode courier
Up and down the convoy
A target, never shot

Leave in Cairo
Bazaar sounds a knife stabbed alien robes
The walk off Crete with your boots on
Dropped rifle, and water bottle
Walking on a march
And you . . . a boy

Sometimes your eyes didn't roll
Eyelids drooped in stillness
To stop our knowing

We're here with you now
In the same room
And know what it was
For you
To live

Closed forever, ol' rolly eyes
I'll remember you
One up, one down.

Hana Te Hemara – Muru Raupatu

I

No more your face
To smile
Life
Without you

No more your voice
To speak and sing
A blessing to weary
Woman, dull soul
Without you

No more you stand
To wave and point
A past whose grief we weep
Without you

No more your balm
To comfort brutal hurt
In violent love's deceit
Without you

So you lay
In stillness
The path where you began
Your ending now
Muru Raupatu

II

Today the earth was put
And rain now comes
To drench the ground
Without my tears, there

Darkness comes between
Your life, this life
A violent knife that cuts
In flashes of glimmer
And steel a lightning edge

Unready and ragged
For life without you
My friend

A clamour of mourning
As droves of voyeurs geeked their fill
Arse turning rude protesting
Petals fell

To the tender stretch of blood
Embracing kinship
Left
Without you

Your frailty
Land
Muru Raupatu

Plans for Christmas

Fish and chips on the beach
Will do
Ay

Could go to Sally's, but
She and the kids'll be with her parents

Could go to May's
She'll be with her kids

Elsie gives me a few bob
From time to time
Could go to her

Or might go north
Hitch
Car's got no reggo

Go and see Matiu
He's got plenty of smoke
Housing Corp took his house
Find out from his brother
Where he is

But I could stay here
. . . wait for May
Then go north
On her car

Otherwise
I'll have fish and chips on the beach
That's okay
Ay

VASA LEOTA

A Kiss

smooth
wet with the freshness
and sweetness of a
flower

IONA LEVI

Born in 1971 in Samoa, Iona Levi attended Samoa College before moving permanently to New Zealand in the 1980s. He considers himself an amateur poet and gains a lot of his inspirational topics from past life experiences. He is currently completing a BA at the University of Auckland.

Holiday Camp

Around the cycle routine – I can heck
are you my friend or just pretend
who you with, red or black?
South side with a posse act
pact with a SOLE attitude
take you out but never rude
stash 3 o'clock screw

6 am start, smoke up large
drag your raggedy ass for porridge gas
standover tactics buy you bread and butter
take it further and you's the man
cobra reflex your survival kit
one man gang or join the clan

10 min lock up was the tune
night cap fix / potent home brew
Polynesian flavour to pull you back
you got problem? Nah I'm cool with dat
no communicate just good with hands

Broken falas who bash their mamas
Good time alkies who worship druggies
con professionals with no-good schemes
violent behaviour from hard core crims

time is your buddy to prepare your climb
fortunate the no longer blind
so sad living a lie

Suck it in

Feel the power – sure 'n' pure
molecules to burn igniting the flight
sock it to me, never mind the bite
tears of gain cancels the pain
suck it in

many a run shouts the gun
retrace the tracks for booby crap
what you see is what you bet
the more you put the more you get
suck it in

overall stride please with thought in mind
one way traffic then around the bend
pity no suga to hold your hand
you got to represent – my friend
suck it in

NAOMI LOSCH

Born in Kahuku, Oʻahu, Hawaiʻi in 1945, Naomi Losch received her early education in the sugar plantation community on rural Oʻahu. She is of Hawaiian, Tahitian, Chinese and Haole extraction and graduated from the Kamehameha School for Girls in Honolulu, a school for children of Hawaiian ancestry. She received her BA in Anthropology and MA in Pacific Islands Studies from the University of Hawaiʻi at Mānoa and is currently an Associate Professor of Hawaiian Language at UHM. Naomi has taught Hawaiian language and culture at university level for over 30 years.

Blood Quantum

We thought we were Hawaiian
Our ancestors were Liloa, Kualiʻi and Alapaʻi.
We fought at Mokuohai, Kepaniwai and Nuʻuanu,
And we supported Liliʻulani in her time of need.
We opposed statehood.
We didn't want to be the 49th *or* the 50th,
And once we were, 5(f) would take care of us.
But what is a native Hawaiian?
Aren't we of this place?
'O ko mākou one hānau kēia.'
And yet, by definition we are not Hawaiian.
We can't live on Homestead land,
Nor can we receive OHA money.
We didn't choose to quantify ourselves,

1/4 to the left	1/2 to the right
3/8 to the left	5/8 to the right
7/16 to the left	9/16 to the right
15/32 to the left	17/32 to the right

They not only colonised us, they divided us.

(In 1920, the United States Congress created the Hawaiian Homes Commission Act. Persons of 50 percent Hawaiian blood or more were eligible to lease homestead lots for 99 years at $1 a year. Since then, other programs which have been established to help the Hawaiian people have had the 50 percent blood quantum imposed. 5(f) is a clause in the Admissions Act (for Statehood) which provides for Hawaiians as defined in the 1920 Act. The Office of Hawaiian Affairs (OHA), a multi-million dollar State of Hawaiʻi agency, also has a provision for native Hawaiians as defined in 1920.)

ABIGAIL McCLUTCHIE

Abigail McClutchie was born in Wellington, New Zealand and is of Ngāti Porou and Te Rarawa descent. She was inspired to write by her younger brother Wiremu McClutchie. She was a student of the University of Auckland, in 1995 graduating jointly with a BA and a BCom. She enjoys all sports, whanaungatanga, te reo Maori, reading and has travelled extensively, both nationally and internationally.

Go to the mountains

Go to the mountains
so that you may be cleansed
by the winds of Tāwhirimātea,
and be free.

Go to the sea
so that you may feel the peace
of Hinemoana's song,
and be inspired.

Go to the ngahere
so that you may be revitalised
by the energy of Tane Mahuta,
and be transformed.

Go to the inner source
so that you may listen to the power,
of your inner essence,
and be enlightened.

for **I am** the Godforce within you.
TE AO MARAMA.

BRANDY NĀLANI McDOUGALL

Brandy Nālani McDougall is a poet of Kanaka Māoli, Chinese and Scottish descent, born and raised in upcountry Maui. A 1994 graduate of the Kamehameha Schools, she received her Master of Fine Arts from the University of Oregon. She was the 2002 recipient of the James Vaughan Award for Poetry and has published in literary journals throughout the US. Most recently, she completed a Fulbright Award to Aotearoa/New Zealand, where she conducted interviews on creative development with other indigenous Pacific writers. She plans to use these interviews to begin a creative writing support network for young artists in Hawai'i and throughout Oceania. Her first collection of poetry, *Origins*, is near completion.

Ma'alaea Harbor, Father's Day

My sister and I sit on rocks, watching sails and glass-
bottom boats, but you are nowhere, so we wait.
Waves glide slowly toward us, crash,
then run away, carrying the unstrung lei
we made for you this morning,
little white buds of plumeria, gardenia.
We will stare until they fade, when
we remember more of you and the sea
you loved, what you carried in your pockets:

cloudy shells, hazy beach glass. On our visits
every other weekend, you led us to the beach,
retrieved pebbles, pieces of driftwood,
lifeless angelfish, frail as ashed paper –
whatever the water had enough of, spit out.

Once, a whole bottle, salt-etched green, unbroken,
let sunlight spark a fire in your hands. Over
our young heads – a faint flash – today's sun, falling
fast into the waves, your lei still floating
toward a horizon pierced with the night's first stars.

The Salt-Wind of Waihe'e

In Waihe'e the salt-wind left nothing
of your house but rusted nails, withered wood,
the howl of the ocean and the sun sinking.

For years, you kept up with the repair,
replacing boards and glass, as you thought you should
in Waiheʻe, with its salt-wind. Nothing

could stop you from such rebuilding, nor bring
you in from outside, where you felt your blood
in the ocean's howl, in the light of the sun sinking

beneath the waves. Your daughters watched
through a window, glass hazed by salt. We stood
out of the Waiheʻe wind and felt nothing

near love, the erosion for a windy sea
that kept you, offering only driftwood
in return. For all the ocean's howling,

we could not understand the urgency
of what stung your eyes, grayed your skin, and flooded
you with the Waiheʻe wind, leaving nothing
but our father's howl, your head slowly sinking.

Emma, 1993

Malihini no nā keiki o ka la kou ʻāina ponoʻī iho.
The children of the land are strangers in their own land.
                                    – ʻŌlelo Noʻeau

I used to wake to my mother sitting in the dark,
looking out the open window
at the far harbor lights. She stared

and stared, turning the gold bracelets
with her Hawaiian name in black,
her wrists flashing spark after spark.

I didn't know what this meant,
why she didn't sleep, why
she waited, breathing in the chilly rain.

What I did know, only sounds:
footsteps on the porch, the metal clink
of her bracelets, the swish of her dresses

like wind through the cane field,
my baby sister's soft cries
after the click of closed doors.

But I talk as if she had died, as if
the choice was not hers to make.
Rather, she left.

She chose love,
the kind of coarse sugar, saltwater
to press to her lips. Watch it stream down

her face, her hands, those men, the love
turning and flashing –
the kind daughters can't give.

Bitterness tells me that's how it should be:
a love story about the naupaka blossoms,
two halves of a flower, without

symmetry or completion, separate,
immovable, my harsh longing to last
through hotels, highways and car lots to come.

The Petroglyphs at Olowalu

The highway to Lahaina, newly paved
and lined in paint, curves against the mountain,

its ridges, cutting black against the gray.
Draped in dry grass, windward slopes descend

from a cloudless sky toward Olowalu,
whose pali is sharp, abrupt. Here, the waves

carve tunnels, caves. They've outlived the hands who
pressed the lines of ghosts into the cliff-face:

stiff triangular figures, broad-shouldered,
ancient men, women and children who climb

or fall against the pali wall, buffered
by ocean wind, the salt carried through time.

Tracing the lines those before me began –
their words I ask for, the long work of hands.

Dirty Laundry

My grandfather hangs our 'ohana's clothes,
cool and wet, on the line. He pauses
only to break the sticky bond between
the crumpled ones – whap! He whips them
against the air, a quick flick of both wrists
before he pins them to the cord. He knows
that one pin should hold two pieces
of clothing in its grasp – first, because it can,
and second, because there will be less
to take down when the clothes are dry.

Earlier, he emptied pockets of change,
balls of used Kleenex, and old candy wrappers.
He sorted each piece by color, lights, darks,
and whites, doing each as a separate load –

while in the bathroom, at the sink,
I scrubbed the ones I didn't want him to see
with Woolite. All the dirt from the day before
runs down the drain in a dark, steady stream.
I am still the clean one. No one has to know.

Lei Niho Palaoa

You have lived through decades under glass,
a velvet bust replacing the one
you once held with love. A thousand strands
of our people's hair were given
to plait your chains; a palaoa offered
a tusk for your hook-shaped pendant.

Your crafters chanted prayers as they worked:
measuring each hair, blending each end
into a new braid, searching the bone
for fractures, carving the inverted arc
of your hook. The days they spent show
the generations of knowing your art.

So, sit proudly in your museum room.
Your people will come for you soon.

DAN McMULLIN

Dan Taulapapa McMullin is a Samoan writer from California, living in Apia, Samoa. He was a collaborating writer on the Pacific/Caribbean US territorial book *Resistance in Paradise*, which won the 1999 Gustavus Meyers Humanitarian Book Award, and his fa'afafine video *Sinalela* won the 2002 Best Short Award at the Honolulu Gay & Lesbian Film Festival. Dan is currently working on a novel tentatively entitled "Sina's Salt Water Dream", and also a documentary script about American Samoa for PBS in the US. He is also painting in Apia.

'O Kaulaiku

Tasi	Lua	Tolu
Let's go into the forest.		
	I'm afraid	I'm not afraid.
There are cacao trees with sweet seeds to suck. There are breadfruit trees, which means baking of course. There are plump birds who sing so sweetly you can almost hear them say yes dear.		
There are tiresome vines, and battlements. There are old land mines, with the imperialists' complements. someone There are shattered trees and giant stinging bees.	I'm afraid of dying. I'm afraid of arguments. I'm afraid of mailing postcards. I'm afraid of seeing treetops. I'm afraid of. I'm afraid of.	I'm not afraid of anything. Except when someone is standing in the distance. I'm very afraid of seeing standing in the distance. I'm afraid of that.
And beyond is an old temple.		
	I know the place.	I don't know the place.
	It's forbidden.	Let's go.
It's really just a clearing.	It's evil.	

They used to dance there long ago.	They ate people!	
That's not true. I don't think it's true.		Well, they stopped didn't they?
Oh, let's go.		Oh, let's go.
Tonight.	No.	No.
	We should finish shelling these nuts.	
		It might be fun.
I'm done.	I'm afraid I'm not done.	I'm done.
Let's wait here under this tree.		
	It's getting dark.	
I can hear the ocean.	I can hear the ocean.	I can hear the flying fish.
	What's that thing there?	
It's my grandparents' tombstone. They were buried together. If you stand here at midnight, you can hear them singing hymns. They were a serious couple.		
	I don't want to hear them singing.	I heard someone singing yesterday.
It's dark now.	Let's go back.	
Follow me.		
Let's go.		
		It's sort of dark up here. Darker than I thought.
We're far enough to raise a light. I brought a lamp. Where are my matches?	Where are your matches? It's awfully dark here.	Something big and wet is on my foot.
There. Now we can see the trail well enough.	The light doesn't make me feel better.	It's just a toad.
	The forest doesn't look better by lamplight.	
Can you hear the forest?		

You say that like it was a person.

It's beautiful.

It is a person. I can hear it talking.

Follow me.

I have to be home by a certain time.

Quiet.

I can see the moon.

Let me blow out the light.

It doesn't look like it.

Wait.

The moon is so big.

It looks like it's falling.

You'd almost think it was falling.

It is falling.

The moon is falling.

The moon is falling.

Hold hands!

The moon is falling.

The moon is falling.

Hold hands.

Circle. Circle. Circle. Circle. Circle. Circle.

The air is turning round with bats.

Here is the moon.

There are bats everywhere.

The moon! The moon! The moon!

Circle. Circle. Circle. Circle. Circle. Circle.

The moon!

The Bat

Once upon a time in old Pulotu there were two fa'afafines named Muli and Lolo.
Lolo was pretty but Muli knew how to talk.
Every night they walked the beaches looking for sailors.
In those days everyone in Pulotu was a sailor.
When they found one they had their way with him
because they never did each other:
one of those things.
Afterwards,
because the islands used to be dens of cannibalism,
one of them hit the nodding sailor with a rock,
and they devoured him.
They did this until there were no more young men left on their particular island.
In fact around this time Lolo had really learned everything he would from Muli,
and Muli was starting to desire Lolo,
so they did each other; but afterwards Lolo killed Muli
and devoured him
as people who come to one for advice will.
This act made the gods very angry at Lolo,
so for punishment they turned him into a bat.

For years Lolo flew up and down the beach at night on little leather wings.
And there were no young men
until finally the Americans landed.
Lolo's first white man, still he knew a sailor when he saw one.
Lolo sank his teeth into the sailor's fat neck and the sailor fainted.
Then Lolo drank until he got plump and passed out.
When he woke up he was in a basket aboard ship
and ended up at the University of Minnesota Medical School
where he was given a nice warm cage by a local foundation.

One day
I'm not sure how but I'll let you know,
he escaped.
It was the especially cold winter of '94;
eighteen-ninety-four.
Lolo flew above the buildings
and south over the pale Mississippi landscape.
It was snowing
and everything was white.
Suddenly far below he saw something in black leather.
Flying down he discovered a boot
that some young man had left there the previous summer

along with his glasses and a pair of shorts he had lost along the river bank
while walking to the corner store late one night to fetch a bottle of milk
for the wife and five kids.

By now Lolo's wings had frozen and he was stuck.
He was in love with the black leather boot
although it didn't speak
and he couldn't eat it.
He didn't think he could eat it
and love it.
The snow kept falling
until it covered them both like a blanket.

The end.

MOMOE MALIETOA VON REICHE

Born in Samoa, Momoe Malietoa von Reiche is well known as an artist,
sculptor, photographer, and writer and illustrator of children's books, as well
as being an accomplished poet. She also runs an art gallery in Samoa called
M.A.D.D., where she holds periodic performances in dance drama and hosts
workshops in creative writing for children.

Taxi 2016

I'm glad this taxi
Is without "sound" –
Loud raucous senseless noise they call "music" –
Stretched love songs that leave one puking –
Silently praying for destinations to materialize.
He fans himself like a tourist in plastic shades,
While guiding the dilapidated craft with
One hand, cruising – (he imagines a sleek silver Toyota or
A smooth black Mazda, the town's popular models)
In the back seat
I listen to "sounds" of "without music" in silence. . . .

The doors rattle in confused rhythm
The front tyres thump in rotational unison,
The axle groans like a dead man
At every turn – not full degreed,
The engine sputters in strangulated protest
While the fan belt whines and whinges,
Is listing . . . is giving way to steam –

I am no mechanic, perhaps what I am
Assessing is in the right terms,
I have to be self-righteous or
Like the taxi, this poem drops dead.

Hanging Wish

There is a hanging wish
In every thought, of all
That is unnoticed and uncared for.
Take this morning for instance:
The collusion of night and day
Invests in the coolness of leaves
While the sour smells of yesterday
Dissipate with quiet rain –
The fiery dews on gardenia
Exude sensuous flavours
Like the unravelling of a lover's treasures –
The immortal fragrance of jasmine
That peep whitely over these hedges
Caress tissues of thoughts
Like soft kisses on the soul.

Once Shadowed by Moons and Children

A tree has many branches
Reaching into the air –
Catching stillness in that pure silence
Once married to the rawness of nature.
Water trickled drops
Leak through light into empty
Spaces once shadowed by

Moons and children –
Like leaves that weave mysteries
The tales that are told in this
Silence, bounce off rusted roofs.

There is undefined beauty here
That seeps out of the roots rattling
And singing –
If she doesn't want to know
Perhaps the sun will.

A Sensuous Tangle With an Incognito Politician

What prompted a
Sensuous tangle with an
Incognito politician in the moonlight
Of Lauli'i – were
Remembrances of promises
Made after a heated night
At Jerome's Cove…
Where the floorboards squealed
With pain and delight
Keeping time with the crescendo
Of Jerome's love lilts, and the
Rhythm of Malekula's guitar.

That pulu tree with an immoral
Canopy of green green leaves
Has eyes that see all –
The sagas that are told and retold
In the retaliatory soul destructive
Repartees of early morning.
Oh, those devoted lovers, forever faithful
Forever truthful,
Rush home with the dawn
To devoted wives.
Misspent moneys, misspent efforts.
In the end
It is all blamed on the music.

SELINA MARSH

Selina Tusitala Marsh was born in Auckland, New Zealand in 1971 and is of Samoan, Tuvalu, German and English descent. Her doctoral research at the University of Auckland explores the works of the first Pacific Islands women to have their poetry published in English. She won a Fulbright Scholarship in conjunction with an East–West Center Award to further her research at the University of Hawai'i at Mānoa, for 18 months. Her poetry has appeared in *Mana* and *Wasafiri*.

afa kasi

afa kasi
half caste
cast in half
a loaded past
carved in half
halved and calved
into one or the other
but neither
is either
full
nor half
       caste
and dyed
       cast
and died
       as different

protest

the text *(kissed)*
      the text *(kissed)*
            the text *(kissed)*
                the text *(kissed)*
the test
      the test
            the test
                the test
the text *(kissed)*
      the text *(kissed)*
            the text *(kissed)*
                the text *(kissed)*
                    of her protest
suckles
      nestles
            suckles
                nestles
the text of her protest
the test of her protest
the sex of her protest
suckles
      nestles
            suckles
                nestles
                          the text of her protest suckles at
                              her breast.

JEAN TEKURA MASON

Jean Tekura Chapman Mason was born on the island of Rarotonga in the Cook Islands. Her mother is a Maori of Ma'uke and Atiu descent. Her father, who migrated from Britain as a child, was a naturalised New Zealander. Jean was educated in the Cook Islands and New Zealand. She is an officer in the Cook Islands Parliament. In 2000 Mason co-edited an edition of *Mana – Cook Islands Special*, an anthology of Cook Islands writing, and in 2001 she published *Tatau*, her first collection of poems. She is married and lives on Rarotonga.

Homecoming

He was just a child,
Your eldest,
When he was stolen
By blackbirders
Carried away
To the Great Southern Land.
You cried and cried
Sorry for a parent's scolding,
Even sent someone
In search of him
But where do you start looking
In the big red country?
150 years later he has returned
In the blue-eyed blonde
Who sits on the uruātete
Where you used to sit
Waiting for him to return
The trade winds are
Your welcoming embrace,
The kuriri sing
Your song of turou
As they fly past.

'Homecoming' is about Taura (Patrick Quinlivan), a Ma'uke boy who, aged about 11, was taken or stowed away to Australia in 1854. He was raised by a Catholic priest whose name he took. He married and settled in Coff's Harbour. His many descendants include the Bardens, Paynes, Masons and Aylings of Western Australia, NSW and Queensland. He is mentioned in the first chapter of Dick Scott's book Years of the Pooh-Bah.

Ancestral Burial Grounds

Ancestors are buried all around us –
Bones liquefied in limestone caves at Ngaputoru
Sun-bleached on sandy shores of 'Avaiki-raro,
Crumbled into dust blown by the marangai;
Bodily essences drained through a pa'ata
Collected for anointment at some mystical rite
At 'Iva, they lie in unmarked graves
Beneath the ocean-waves of Te Moana-nui-o-Kiva.

Trees and rocks are their markers,
Mountain caves their mausoleums, no family crypts at 'Araki,
Nor tidy sum spent at Parkinson and Bouskill
For odes on stone or seraphim singing their praises,
Just their voices in the wind
Whispering karakia in ancient Maori,
Names in a tattered puka papa'anga
Bestowed upon a newborn child,
And the echoes of their footsteps
On the time-worn pathways we now tread.

Ma'uke Childhood

Where rock-daisies stalked
The thicket like tigers
Burning brightly in the grass;

Where a swim in the water
Of cool chasm-pools
Was heaven after a hot day's play;

Where ni'oi leaves
And the ubiquitous kikau
Was a jew's harp in our mouths and hands;

Where the sweet scent of mata'oi
Intoxicated all our senses
In the bright afternoons;

Where we scraped our knees and hearts
In the makatea chasing mene'une in the flowers
Of the crawling pumpkin vine;

Where our chins and memories were indelibly
Stained by cashew-apples on our way home
From 'Araro;

Where time-worn limestone trails
Behind grandfather's house
Were aglow with spectral fishermen
Dragging their paiere down to the sea at night.

Where my child with the blue eyes
Sparkling like jewels on the ocean
Plays on the shining sand
Where once I played.

. . . will the land of my tupuna consume her
like it does me?
. . . how can I forget it even in my dreams?

TRIXIE MENZIES

Trixie Te Arama Menzies was born in Wellington in 1936 and lives in Auckland
with her husband Barry Menzies. She is of Tainui and Scottish descent. She has
three adult children, five surviving grandchildren, two great-grandchildren and
several mokopuna atawhai. She has taught at secondary schools in Auckland
and at the University of Auckland. Her four poetry collections are *Uenuku*
(Waiata Koa, 1986), *Papakainga* (Waiata Koa, 1988), *Rerenga* (Waiata Koa, 1992)
and *In the Presence of My Foes* (Waiata Koa, 2000). Together with Ramai Te Miha
Hayward, the late Arapera Hineira Kaa Blank, Toi Te Rito Maihi and others,
Trixie is a founding member of Waiata Koa, a Maori Women's Artists and Writers
Collective, which was formed at the time of the Karanga exhibition in 1986.

Muka

To the weavers of Waiata Koa

So may I be as the muka –
My flax has been patu'd by stone pounders
I am dyed in the colours of my passions

but then taken and shaped by deft loving fingers
of the master craftswomen,
disciplined into design

At the last, may I shine lustrous with inner fires
which were fed through green blades
from the body of Papatūānuku
alight with radiance of Te Rā,
fitted to serve

Uenuku

Out from the unencompassed past you stand
Beaming your radiance on us, Rainbow-named
Stranger to time yet owning those your kin
Who flank you, softer spirals to your spines,
Their fingers locked inside their rounded forms
Who was the bold one turned yours round, up, free?
Body reaching out from embedding wood
Sends the bands arcing in defiant waves;
Visible spectrum spans a watery sky,
Combs out its ghostly locks by mirrored light,
Watches the gathering masses from on high

Uniquely formed, inscrutable response –
Rejecting questions that enquire too close.
But to all those protected by that power
Such secret knowledge may we feast on there
That we too may float free and walk the air.

Ki Āku Tipuna Māori

Where are my people of the tōnuitanga
I have shared the love-hate politicking of the family –
Once there was a whanau but we are separated –
Ka raungaiti au.

Once there was a black-eyed woman who was my ancestress,
She lurked behind the innocent eyes of my babies,
In the sweaty beds of love she was the one I sought but did not know it.
I never heard her name, this forgotten woman

She was my blood my bone my pulse my smell my breath
When I first danced with death she was my chaperone
Later to be unmasked as procuress.

Sometimes I sense her in a patch of garden,
A place where crops grow by themselves unplanted
Or a certain stretch of coast touched by a warm late season.

Worms gnaw her bones as one day they will gnaw at mine
When I find where she lies, there would I lie contented.

Watercress

We sensed the place from fifty yards
As we passed the white upstanding trees,
Then walked along the railway, on the sleepers,
Or holding hands to balance on the lines
Charcoal rock intruded under our feet
Gorse interfered on the side
We knew the storm was coming, by the wind and the oddly yellow light
But we thrust through the gorse to the fence
Tearing up young puha shoots as we went
To go with the watercress we hoped to find.
You said, dreamily, this doesn't look like watercress country
But we spotted the barrow, a small swelling
As if the earth was trying to hide something under her coat
I was embarrassed at intruding on something private
I felt I should walk away
Burnt gorse and manuka, and a cabbage tree
With the first peal of thunder we were knee-deep in mud and watercress
We filled out kit, letting the rain soak us
Searching the mound for bogs, penetrating the earth's secret places
Feeling in each patch of mud for food.

KARLO MILA

Karlo Mila was born in 1974 and is the daughter of Maka Ulu'ave Mila and Lynda Hunt. Of Tongan, Palagi and Samoan descent, Karlo grew up in Palmerston North and works in Auckland as a Manager for Pacific Health Research. She has written poetry all her life, mostly to capture people she honours (and the politics of relationships) on paper.

Our mother is in love

You are so busy giving him the best of you
we are left with the scraps
fry up, boil up, bubble and squeak
we are throwing you to the birds

you are a partner now
            a part of someone else
all we have
are your lukewarm leftovers
we are throwing you to the birds

we are feeding you to the cat

WORD combinations/mutations:
wheelbarrow, howl, pumpkin, wretched, shred

a)
he is pushing a wheelbarrow loaded with slaughter
serial killer savouring the sexy scent of death
not a shred of mercy for the stems bleeding
and the hibiscus howl through their thin yellow mouths
bruised pumpkin petals weeping, wretched

b)
the chip on your shoulder is so big
you need a wheelbarrow
i have shred my anxieties into small ribbons

i wear gaily in my hair and sip pumpkin soup
think of you wretched and howl with laughter

c)
we shred each other into pieces with our long nails of love
you left me scabby and howling and wretched
plant your own garden, a wise person said,
instead of waiting for someone to bring you flowers
wheelbarrow in hands, I plan to plant pumpkins instead
to sustain me through a winter without you

d)
the wheelbarrow we bought together lies rusting on its side
the pumpkins we planted went to seed through neglect
the wind howls and our wretched little trees shed their leaves gracelessly
as if knowing there is now only an audience of one
violets grow like small gifts through the weeds
tender shreds of what we once hoped for

For John Pule

the poet told us
there was a beach
but a hurricane came
and swallowed it up

there was also a nation of people
but a New Zealand sponsored
hurricane
just as hungry
swept away people like grains of sand

with the help of
longremembered newfound family
he finds the old foundations
where hibiscus trees grow wild
with memories of his mother

using a new machete
he follows the old tracks

to a not so distant past
meeting his ancestors along the way
capturing them on canvas
mapping out their stories
so they will
never be lost

and his own children
will be able to find them

For my mother

I have to ask
what was a nice girl like her
doing in her life
living in that house
living as his wife

a middleclass girl
a methodist girl
with a dead father
whose ideals
she hoped to live up to
impossible task
pregnant with me

I can see you at playcentre
long dark hair
      centre part
           skivvy
              batik skirt
golden ring where it should be (somewhat belatedly)

but
white girl
are they your caramel children?
on your hips
      holding your hands
          on your shoulders
a nice girl like you?

and he labours
literally
brown bread
winner

so proud of his palagi wife
his palagi life

the divorce is to be expected really
new respectable blond husband
the caramel children have turned to custard

recently

I have been seeing you
in other people's faces
 in my cousin's smile
            in the eyes of the nurse on the bus
                    in the kaumatua's tongue
            as he flicks saliva over his lips

it is some trick of light and flesh and eye and mouth

and I recall the last time I saw you
as you stamped your well heeled foot
on the floor
for the first time I noticed the cloven hoof
as you threw back your black mane of hair
                            and laughed
I watched your nostrils flare
and realised you weren't quite
                    human
and what remained of my heart
I scraped off your shoe
and swallowed quickly
hoping it wasn't too late for me

I haven't seen you since
        except for flickers in my cousin's smile
                glints in the eyes of the nurse on the bus
                    and in the kaumatua's tongue

as he flicks it over dry lips
and nervously
breaks the bad news

Wednesday afternoon

my father is "having fun"
cleaning the floor
he uses the plugged in sink as a bucket
wears rags on his feet
and shimmies to a cleaning beat
he asks me to read the label
on the bottle for him
he wants our floor to shine
and laughs when (surprise)
it does
this is how I will remember him
moonwalking across our kitchen floor
rags under his feet
"that's how my mother taught me"
he says
"but I never take any note
it takes me forty years to do what she say"

KELLYANA MOREY

Born in 1968 and of Ngāti Kuri, Te Rarawa and Te Aupouri descent, Kellyana Morey spent much of her childhood in Papua New Guinea. She has a BA in English and an MA specialising in contemporary Maori art, and she is currently undertaking an M. Litt. Her story, "Maori Bread", featured in the first *Tandem 100 Short, Short Stories* anthology and "The Gardenia Tree" is found in the fourth edition of the same series. In 1997 her story "Tangiweto" was a finalist in the Huia Maori Writing Awards. In recent times Kellyana's interest has turned to the novel and she is working on a trinity of novels called "Bloom", "Monsoon" and "Waiting". She is a graduate of the University of Auckland creative writing class.

ture te haki

. . . you fly your flags of history quietly
for now
battle pendants hidden in wooden boxes
in blackened rooms
rotting and fading into dust under
well intentioned eyes
that wonder at your beauty and your stories and
your size
no land beneath the wool and cotton
and silk
the star of David, the cross of Mikaere and the
wounded heart
bleeding
no way for you to come home
you sit and wait for darkness to go quickly
for light to fall on your ruined threads
the flags are quiet
for now . . .

The Islands

There is a map on the wall of my room.
Longitude and latitude
scar swept and sweetly over
the Islands.
Tracing the topography
pausing where the lines transect and
become one.
The geography of blood and tissue
collapsing under greedy fingers.
Spine bent skyward in the
vagaries of lassitude.
These shores taste of humming birds before
the bite.
The cartographer has drawn the way there on
my parched skin costume.
I scrub at it with navigator eyes.
The shortest way home, as the crow flies.

Cartography

The desire to map is unexplained nurture
that devoured, then manifested
itself
at the very core of how we examined
the boundaries we so carefully
defined.
Bent
deliciously sun drenched
towards waiting land
response being heart drunk and nature
inherent.
To watch
the contradictions of faith
from another
tower.
Taking whole
every ounce of being
in a mouthful as large as the doors of a church.
Recognising the futility

in the way of recalling
because forgetting is as easy
as remembering
most days.

LOA NIUMEITOLU

Loa Niumeitolu was born in 1970 in Kolomotu'a, Tonga. Loa has returned to
Tonga after a 15-year absence in the USA and is now the organiser of Mataliki
Tonga Writers' Group and other creative activities in the community. Loa writes:
"Creativity is so formalised in Tonga, which is wrong because to sincerely create is
to survive and celebrate living and everyone is entitled to that."

When we tell

I know English was brought
by White people to our country.
But when WE speak it,
when we slur that language like sinews
of vine floss extracting our teeth,
grind it with coral and ironwood in our mouths.
When WE tell of the gritty taste,
we've got to have a Tongan way
of doing it.

Tuitui

Touching, holding the trunk
of our coconut,
patting the tufts of moss
climbing its back.
Feeling the light breathing
of coldness in May.

Our gods talking,
we're startled by fleeting birds.

What does it mean when the mei
sheds its rusty leaves quicker
than the moko regrows?

Watch me . . .

What does it mean when
the daughter who loves you
is silenced by the sting of your palm
on her face?

For the siale to open in abundance
you must witness words, steaming out
from lungs of restless boys,
burning under light post shadows
of bold girls who laugh their steam
like over boiling the teapot.
The frothy white blossoms
brown as the kaloni kakala
climbs its trellis and rests
on pua trees and walkways.

Out of this, something is being said.

Have you sat on the calf of the old ovava,
just above the knotted ankle?
Hung on to its brooding beard?

A god dropped a tuitui,
you picked it up, cracked it, chewed it
with mohokoi into a lather –
your knowledge of home.

I'm talking to the child in our bellies,
almost ripe.

No, Tukulaumea, it's not for you to be
confused with who is the god?
What is the god?
Where is the god?

See . . .

The same tuitui stands, the one we gathered
lather from when my mother was young.

Rub your bodies,
it smells of petals, bark, hard nut, heavy rain,
breezes of salt, milk, earth.

It is a fananga, a riddle, a way of life.
It is a god, our knowledge
                our resistance,
                the lather of the tuitui
                steaming on our skin.

MICHAEL O'LEARY

Born in Auckland, New Zealand, Michael John O'Leary is of Irish and Te Arawa
descent. He has a BA from Otago University and an MA from Victoria University
of Wellington. He is a writer, researcher and publisher, and currently lives in
Paekakariki. He has written articles and stories for newspapers and journals, and
reviewed books for both the *New Zealand Listener* and the *Sunday Star Times*. His
publications include collections of poetry (*Ka Atu I Koopua*, 1999 and *T.A.B. Ula
Rasa*, 2001), novels (*Out of It*, 1987 and *Straight*, 1984) and works of history (*Gone
West, a history of Auckland's Waikumete Cemetery*, 1985 and *Grafton Cemetery*, 1984).
His latest book of poetry *Toku Tinihanga* (Selected Poems 1982–2002) is due for
publication by HeadworX in 2003.

Kia Aroha rua

we sat silent at the foot
of the poet's statue
I had put my coat around you
to keep off the southern evening coldness
and, with my arm around your shoulder
we waited
for the time we would no longer be together

which came soon enough –
as your husband's car came to a stop
at the traffic lights
my arm moved instinctively away
and the seeds of the trees
which necessarily separate us
are again planted

but each time
we are apart we grow together
like an unseen river
beneath the surface of our lives
the aroha
is between us
as well as the distance

and that evening
we had laughed and danced, sang
and talked of death and darkness and light
the best thing was that we were happy
as we walked from the restaurant
to sit silent at the foot
of the poet's statue

For my Father in Prison, 1965

Doing time
        my father would have needed time to do this

To build a table
        made from matchsticks, our only family heirloom

Matchstick upon
        matchstick held together with some kind of glue

Just like the
        brick building which held him

Yes, that's it
        stone upon black stone which kept him captive

He entered through
        the heavily bolted steel door they held open

And when he emerged
      he had a matchstick table and was very quiet

Each matchstick
      represented a fragment of his life

Each fragment
      was there outside him, set in a glue and he was a shell

Poem to your Grandmother

i

digging up the ground
so that her lifelong partner
could rest with her
    they found
her long long silver hair
    pride of her womanhood
had tangled round and round
the root of a breadfruit
              tree
in time, without a sound
woman and tree had merged
she had become nature
out of sight, underground

ii

but, as though to stake his claim
and make her not forget him – not
for something so simple as a breadfruit
                tree
her, her human love – I'll say husband
had died
    could only live one year without her, rather
and her breadfruit tree had to give her up

iii

a tree grows on a mound
of earth, under which he and she lie
in death as they had done in life,
together now without a sound
woman and man and tree have merged
have become nature hair and root and heart
out of sight, underground

Noa / Nothing I (an irony)

Rightfully, these words should not be making their way across the page because I am nobody. I have no name and I have no whanau, I am a fragment, the lost piece of a jigsaw. Without mana, without kaha, without children to continue me, I only live. Kei te noa, ahau. Nothing I. Every word I speak scatters to the wind and is heard only as a sound with no meaning. I have no taste, no smell, no movement. Unseen, I am not even like the invisibility of salt in a pot of cooking potatoes. Only the darkness knows who I am and silently laughs. Hine nui te pō sits waiting. Haurangi, pōrangi – any rangi! Shattered visions permeate my days. When the rangi of me cries and the seeds grow within papa, that's the only time of connection and a sadness comes from the only belonging. I am of te rangi and I cannot see or hear the sound of the sea; I am of te hau and I cannot move; I am of te ao and I cannot touch a thing.

TIM PA'U

Tim Pa'u was born in New Zealand in 1962, of Samoan and German descent. After leaving school Tim worked at various jobs then for small newspapers in Hamilton and doing freelance work in Auckland before going to Samoa with his twins. While working for the *Samoa Observer*, the national English newspaper, Tim suffered a serious beating. When he recovered, he returned to New Zealand and worked in various rest homes. He started his BA at the University of Auckland in 1998, and will complete his degree at summer school 2002–2003, with a major in English and a minor in History. Tim intends continuing his studies and will enrol for his BA (Hons) in 2003.

That path he travelled!

left
for
dead
on
side
of
road
head beaten to a pulp, stepped outside code
back home from night out, feed from Makeki

o la	Meet
se	Apia's
faasiga	'fai
au	leo
because	leo
of	sa
palati	oka
sikaleti	se
	moepi

..........drunken state, o la se aisi tupe ma sikaleti, e lema

instant
verbal
abuse   one
"kefe   against
lou   five

a
lelo"
ha!
ha!
ha!

"fasioti
na
niu
Sila
Pepelo"

Contrary to belief, he fights hard and long
Hockey stick ma steel bar cements their strong
he
lucky
masani
laititi
oti
leilei
they
not
know
toe
alive
again
another
day

sapose to pi me pro!

acknowledings – nah
highs fives – nah
introductions – nah
smiles – yo!
casual starings – yo!
Putt prada I wish u be my pro!
howevers your foliga say no!
maype I's full of assumptions
maype I's too old
maype I's not kools enuf
putt if you poots your hand in the hands
of the manz
I bromise – friends for eva
friends for lifes.

NZ Born

English
             First language
culture
             Palagi style
fanku – fuck – le faa Samoa
difficulty sorting new cultural identity
labelled / hate labels

own person – unique's
many a cultural mistake along way
older – more into home culture
Samoan – not Maori or Raro
Spell the name write
into POLICE, RADIO HAURAKI, no accent
                      dead give away
fashion, desire, lifestyle
                      dead give away
but slow – slouch – too casual
                         can't be
good English, broken Faa Samoa
                         can be

Disgrace

Auckland University – teach, be Samoan supporter
               for Maori rights
Waitangi Treaty – shame! shame! shame!
colonisation – blame! blame! blame!
Heke & Ratana – heroes for all time
Republicanism come soon for da
                    Tagata Whenua!

BRIAN POTIKI

Born in New Zealand in 1953 into the Kāi Tahu, Kāti Māmoe tribe, Brian lives
in Rotorua. He has just completed a historical play/trilogy (*A Mutiny Stripped,
Boultbee, Hiroki's Song*) set in the South Island and is also working on a book
about the play, *Maranga Mai*, a seminal work of Maori theatre, 1980–81, which
he directed, co-wrote and acted in.

tai tokerau daughter

the marae tilting
a pukeko's black house
orange in the flames
everyone
crying

huhana oneroa get up!
you were only fortyseven
whaddya doin wrapped in
wood, tapa, clay
mud
(apart from goin round n round?)

remembering our last day
you leaning in the car window
asking if I had any
smoke

I poured all I had
in my little tin
into your
hands

your hands
where'd they go?

tony

tony it's me at the gate
with some mussels &
a dozen beer in a crate.
i see a te whiti miniature
on the easel,
your own body dipped in ink
from samoa.
i'm with you tony!
on a cliff face at muriwai
with emily karaka in a storm

& finally

at the coffin
alan is kissing your face
(makeup running all over the place)
just as you kissed phil clairmont's eyes
back then.
another coffin,
same passion.

what police

(for gerry)

what matter if the paper in this typewriter
be straight or strait?
who cares? what police?
bob in *metro* (the one with
the cricketer patel on the cover):
inside sad-faced bob. sad for all the world.
who all the doctors-without-degree chided
to "put de bung back in de bottle shipmate".
yesterday bob sent me a book of lorca's letters.
in it are photos of anteater-faced neruda,
also lorca the year before he was killed
(looking like brendan behan).
in one letter lorca is rushing to new york
to the house of a professor of spanish
& yearning to drink cognac there

in my caravan are books,
all with exciting titles & script.
they are my undersea world!
sometimes i perfume the air with jazz or soul –
the duende of black men & women

meanwhile the coffee staining my gums
and racing my heart.
but. what police. eh?

ROMA POTIKI

Born in Lower Hutt, New Zealand in 1958, Roma Potiki's tribal affiliations
are to Te Rarawa, Te Aupouri and Ngāi Rangitihi. She is a playwright and com-
mentator on Maori theatre, as well as a theatre performer and manager, who was
Te Toka-a-Toi (Maori arts) co-ordinator of the 1998 New Zealand International
Festival of the Arts. Roma is also a visual artist, who illustrated her own first
collection of poems and has work in the permanent collection of the Dowse
Gallery, Lower Hutt. Her published poetry includes *Stones in Her Mouth* (1992)
and *Shaking the Tree* (Steele Roberts, 1998), and her work has been widely
anthologised.

when it's summer

when it's summer
and earth and sky almost meet
i lie down, stomach-up on the sand dunes

bare skin
and sun
and the sea lifting
and pressing down on sand.

and even though my eyes are closed i feel the imprint of the
season
the wash of light and heat on my lids.

relaxing
i breathe in the saline breath of Tangaroa
smell the pumice and earth mingling.

and it's all sensation
as i stand and run down to the sea, to the water.
feel its kick and rhythm
its fish music.

buoyant and strong i am carried back
to the lip of firm sand.

foam loops over my ankles
i smile and dig my hands in.

a chant for 19 women murdered

please won't you get out before he kills you
please won't you get out while you can
cause there's already been 19 women murdered
by husbands who said they loved them

he rapes you, but you don't call out
cause you don't wanna wake the kids in the back room.
one day they won't wake you
gone with a man the same as him
in a house with no music
and every regret.

you can't save him
though he'll try to convince you
it's just words
just another bottle, just another fight
just another fist in the middle of the night.

you're tired, close to falling
so, please won't you get out before he kills you
please won't you get out while you can
cause there's already been 19 women murdered
by husbands who said they loved them.

cycle of five poems

Sulphur
a full breast to the moon
misty sulphur beats around the candle flame
and submerged in grey silk
i stretch full length and keep afloat

outside the pool i feel the full weight of you inside me
still alive

inside the flat is a bed and a book

Ika
my stomach is pulled tight now
heavy sand, before the tide
breathing is difficult.

gasping fish swim past enormous rocks
and out to deeper water.
the little passage grows large
then closes again.
ika does not look back.

beached mucus dries and is returned to the land.
the little ika swims harder.

For Tarawera
out of the shadows
out of the gloom
it was a rare rolling baby
eyes cast wide
magic magic, ferns 'n' hot tides
magic, magic, fishes' eyes!

Late nights with baby
you bloody try writing at 3am
with a baby on one breast, and biting
a pen in my left hand, stumblegaited it to the toilet.
sitting beneath an unsubdued light
emblazoned, red-eyed and breathless
a blank, bleary beauty.

Babies sleep
babies sleep
babies sleep
he dreams all the things he'll ever be.
hands touch the night
lightly, lightly
he's asleep.

Toetoe Turn

Moon cloaks
pale and incandescent
waving above the bedroom window.

Toetoe rains,
falls down
drifts of wheaten silver, just-born green & yellow
the occasional umber-touched shower
and the traditional golden stem,
thin and proud in the night.

I dream of old women marching,
they hold the toetoe, toetoe above them –
in a procession they walk the earth
up the hills
to the meeting places
the heaving rocks
where she&he she&she he&he might be found.

Usually it is dusk or dark or dawn.

I have not seen them move together in the day
yet.

Torches flame the nightly light,
some say even the surface of rivers and lakes can show
the path.
Stumbling forward, or sedate and vaguely safe within
the known group,
striking out or treading slowly,
we hear we smell we see and sense
where we will move.

Moonstone & feathers
pāua and crab
mussel and tuatua
pipi and pupu and oyster.

Toetoe, flax-seed
pīngao and ti-kōuka

all these adorn the cloak
I wear.

My mother, my father
leaders of the monumental procession –
each in turn, the moon's rotation.

Flight

We have flown halfway round the world
to stand among lions.

They face us
stone and chiselled granite
the grins of an empire
holding the keys to a house of treasures.

We have been lovingly fitted into
a small room
but a small room it is
and in this space the red kōkōwai spills
and flies its angled journey above our heads
as karakia move amongst old ones
from a time that grows closer as we visit the past.

Red kōkōwai and suddenly
the room fills with the movement of the sea,
forests and tupuna sighing and whirling slowly above us.

I close my eyes –
no Jesus in the temple
no exchange of money.

A bird spills ochre from its loving beak.
A gift to encourage the many journeys
of return.

JOHN PULE

John Pule was born in 1962 on the family land of Pia in the village of Liku on Niue. He arrived in Aotearoa/New Zealand in 1964 and held a number of labouring jobs before he started writing poetry in 1980. He has published poetry and prose, and his publications include *Winter, The Rain* (Fragrance on Earth Press, 1981), *Sonnets to Van Gogh* (FOE, 1982), *Flowers After the Sun* (FOE, 1984), *The Bond of Time* (FOE, 1985), *The Shark That Ate the Sun* (Penguin, 1992), *Burn My Head in Heaven* (Penguin, 1998), and *Bond of Time* (Pacific Writing Forum, USP, Fiji, 1998). He received the Pacific Island Arts Award in 1996, was Writer in Residence at the University of Waikato in 1996, Writer in Residence at the Pacific Writing Forum, University of the South Pacific in 1997, Artist in Residence at the Oceania Centre for Arts & Culture, USP, Fiji and at the University of Canterbury during 1998, and Writer in Residence at the University of Auckland in 2000. John is a full-time artist and poet.

14

I woke up to find a butterfly across your mouth
you were dressed in those oriental jackets
which tricked me into believing dragons sufficed
so I scrawled a poem onto the wall

how I reached these shores on the *Maui Pomare*
some white girl, impressed with what I wrote
tore the wallpaper off and ran, I watched
as she ran with maps and charts to my destination

I called out, only half of me belongs here,
she stops, looks back, deep in thought, what do you mean,
she replies, thinking twice about the wallpaper

the land, as I walk towards her, and how
it does not decide who should die or be buried,
before I reach her, only words remained of her flight

6

My heart longs to touch you
to hear you like I hear children
this voice of mine will rise and sing with
the impeccable things that come from you

upon your bronzed beautiful skin
like on the shore of a magnificent sea
I'll watch the pohutukawa red
in the brilliant distant of your eyes

to lay close to you would be lying
upon a field of jasmine and daffodils
to smell the fragrance of the sea on
your belly, and sleep and sleep

your body is the colour of moth and pear
coconut picked by a Polynesian
the colour of the lush south island
potato, thrush, copper and gold vase

9

I am a great liar
my thoughts are pure truth
My voice is a liar
I ask for your forgiveness

Tonight I keep no past
from you, my life is only
years of time and mortality
an emigrant, a uga

speaking of my life is giving
your lips for me to kiss
falling over the boat's rail
two years old holding onto a white hand

That is life, born in another spirit
knowing objects that had no form
flesh, born on another land,
that is life, I keep no past from you

The Hurricane Love Songs

1.

I now chance the night to write a song
that wanders in the personality of mist
koromiko slipping out of unwanted clothes
drops of water shaped like lit candles

If I was
If I was to tell you
If I was to tell you that I was born without
a bird pecking at my teeth, the kowhai
at the precious windows, a field of yellow
light and jocular roads ending at my eyes
would you believe me?

Then it is settled
I came to these shores barely able to reach the belly
of my mother.
My feet already clad in soil with
a history of the koho and the smell of tyres,
a futureless beach at the end of the journey
a junction full of ships and floral dresses
as I am carried off the vessel
to stand on a platform rained on in the night.

I have since studied my hands
one side is white as the moon
a soft illusion curled at the lips
the other side is dark as your eyes

Never mind I keep telling myself
I have grown up here in a certain uncomfortable space
my shadow casts a question on the secret air
If I should drop everything I had found at the door

Ocean Song to Myself

when the soul has been wounded and the sun is keen
to surface in the dark there is one place I go to
that place that fills the earth's land with moisture and
water, that changes the coast in a dream, that place
the ancients call mother of mothers, the ocean

there along the sand soft as illusions, sparkles with
stars, the white shells sculptured by mouths of
myth and minerals, and touches deep whirls of death while
fish fly towards the breaks, and foam collects sadness
of if the horizon perpetuates eternity and a wave
samples marine change, then I baptise myself, sing to
myself, sing to the ocean, and the cold faith
dive into time memorial, safe as blood, knotted to
the nakedness, crying to the sea, open to
the glowing extreme, and ecstasy, in a state
of sleep, so nothing solid drifts too far
for queries is the soul's intention.

when I emerge from myself to learn the language
allegorised by twenty-eight years of dreaming, senses
take on the appearance of trees to wind up their
song among the birds for the leaves sing a tune misled
by ships, or whales mating, moving depths to drift
to caves, and watch fossils lost in the legs of
gannets feeding their chicks.

gannets strike a musical chord for traces of religious
visions, to cover wounds that go away briefly
to pray darkness or grieve, but return
likes waves to eat at united entities, so I stand
in the ocean, recite my whakapapa, first to the north
where I tasted timala and dirt
to the west, the east and the south.

I mix my tears with the salt and the waves, drink a cup
so the veins are fattened with life
when life flees from the body we must sing it back
rituals and internal prayers
for the sun's acute dedication to the flower petals
we become humble and embrace, we lose

the knowledge.
I kneel in the surf and trust the ocean to take me
but not take me, to show her wrath by
playing, and then seal the light that escapes
from the wound that lovers call lips
I walk out and the rocks remain quiet as a moon.
Pohutukawa and puriri dance in the noonday sun
pukeko chase my shadow into the mountains
as the clouds that follow the time of never returning
goodbye.

PRISCILLA RASMUSSEN

Born in New Zealand in 1969 to Samoan parents from the villages of Savalalo and Lepea, Priscilla Rasmussen was raised and schooled in the suburbs of Wellington. She studied at Victoria University of Wellington and started writing for the university magazine and community newspapers. After gaining a BA in Education, she continued her studies at the Wellington Polytechnic, gaining a qualification in journalism. She worked as a writer/researcher for TVNZ's *Good Morning*. She left TVNZ after four years to have a baby, then left New Zealand to travel through Asia while working as an English teacher. She is still working and living in North East Asia with her daughter.

Polynesian Poetry . . . (for the anthology)

(clearing the throat and straightening the page)

>   Poetry . . .

>   your languishing lashings of lilting linguistics
>   cools my feverish words
>   that seep
>   at the womb
>   of my intention . . .

>   . . . nope . . .

(moving down the page)

>   Poetry . . .

>   poetry, Polynesians, postmodernism
>   and palms with points
>   picking through our poetry
>   and prose
>   and possibilities
>   with people
>   preparing
>   to
>   pick
>   (or pass on)
>   Poly-filler points
>   for the purpose
>   of

publishing

. . . nah . . .

(changing the page)

Poetry . . .

I read you al
may I call you that?
I feel like
I know you
already

I read you momoe
may I call you?
I feel like
I could
already

I read you konai, sano et al
could I be so bold?
to say I feel
like you
already?

. . . oh dear . . .

your village
your youth
your scholarship days
(and those of your kids)
and homecomings

of fish
and friends
of ghosts
and old men, always
old men

often the rain
sometimes the sea
fanning the moon
born of the land,

always
the land

and dreams

> . . . I can't weave like you do . . .
> the rain on *my* face is . . . wet!

(next page)

Poetry . . .

I read you my contemporaries
you give me mea ai
my sisters in word
consuming your thoughts
of mothers and fathers
fathers and mothers
and the warmth of aiga,
of ritual abuse
lots of
abuse
and
con-
fu-
shun

of home
and chores
and pressure cookers,
in Man-gree
and Noo-town
lotu tamaiti – pese Samoa!
in school with palagi
in school with Ma-oli
in school with
Eh-doo-kay-shun
and pressure,
from
the womb,
always
that
bloody
womb

and

your father's dreams

                                             . . . um . . .

(new page)

growing up

chilly winters
rugby
and *rain*
on netball courts
koko laisa
chops and mash
Samoan roots
and island time
a theatrical mother
redundant father
and a touchy uncle or two (what's new)
favoured brothers
girl cousins as friends, always
as friends
non-working-class neighbourhood
teachers that sneer
"my, that's clever for a brown girl, dear"
Living a dichotomy
1. Kia ora bro from Wainui
2. E te mana'o i se ipu ti?
(I've read you too Al-feleki)
you're only a girl, just a coconut, a smart effin' bitch
you got that right!
now feel my might

mighty

mighty

words

                                             . . . hmmmm . . .

(scribbling out the page)

this ain't poetry
it rhymes too much
and it's not PC

too sedimen-ta-ree
rudimen-ta-ree
and full of me
for this anthology
what is poetry?

will

you

read

me?

Over Dinner

she said she was pregnant
I cried in my curry
then ate
the hot
salted tears

her face just shimmered
like my glistening lychees
I glowered
she glimmered
with child

we toasted to babies
to years as cousins
to Fatu
her lover
(and mine)

I started to chuckle
as my tears turned to chilli
the burning
drowning
in wine

I thought of my baby
gone just ten days
a ten-week-old
secret
dissolved

as I finished my curry
I smiled and said yes
to godmother
a mother
no more

VAINE RASMUSSEN

Born on Rarotonga in the Cook Islands in 1961, Vaine began writing both poetry
and short stories at the age of twelve. As she says, "it was an outlet to express
myself because no one was listening to me anyway". She runs her own
consultancy service from Rarotonga, specialising in development and
management advisory services. Her first publication was a collection of poems
entitled *Maiata* and published by the Pacific Commonwealth Youth Program in
Honiara. She is currently working on the publication of a second collection with
the University of the South Pacific.

The Joys of a Working Mother

There are traces of you
When I go to work

– the grubby fingerprints
that enhance the
floral prints on my dress front;

– the lost stapler at last
found wedged between files
in the filing cabinet;

– your toys like land mines
planted strategically at
plodable intervals
in the office

– your matchbox truck
a paper weight
on the desk;

But of all

– your face in my mind and
heart keeping me warm when
I work.

The Sea and Her Delights

I saw scenes of you
in between maneaba eaves
Tantalising images
that whet the soul.

The lagoon abounds with tawatawa
A sign of better things to come.

Your woman warms you
with her body and food

Rebuilding strength
for the fish hunt.

Tonight you sleep

with her
But tomorrow
you are mine
as you glide your
canoe over my
body and find
food for your family in my
arms.

Fishermen of Nareau,
I have never been
unfaithful to you.

Bus ride from Holeva to Neiafu

four stands of kape
separate me from you
I watch you among
your mates and
think of
another young man like
you that I love,
he has a dream
and I'm helping
him make it
come true,
I'm sure
someone's helping
your dreams
it shows on the
pressed school uniform
you wear and
the coconut oil
conditioning your hair.

there is a woman

behind you
making sure your dreams
are met and as your body heat
whiffs the scented oil from
your skin
I am incited with
a warm feeling
of love
for the future
and all
its uncertainties
and the bus
stops at
Vava'u High
and you
alight to
make your dream come
true, and
I continue on
to find a
dream
to do.

TIALUGA SELOTI

Moa

I've known the soul of Moa
Whose blood flows through my veins
And whose mauli is rooted in my heart
Pure and Sacred
E sa oe moa
What do you stand for?
A lifestyle imprint
M O A
Mind Our Aiga
Make our aganu'u
Mould our attitudes
For there once lived
The sacred warrior Moa
Navigator of sea and land
Peopled with his many sons
When brother struck brother
Moa stood in the gap
Moasatuileva
I shall do the same
For you and I are heirs of Moa
Members of the family of
Samoa

LUAFATA SIMANU-KLUTZ

Luafata Simanu-Klutz was educated in Samoa and New Zealand in the 1960s and 1970s and has been living in Honolulu since 1986. A teacher by profession, she has taught elementary classes in New Zealand, Apia, and American Samoa. Since migrating to the United States, Luafata has been involved in inservice teacher training, multicultural education, and school improvement in the American Pacific. Currently, she is completing a doctoral degree in Pacific History at the University of Hawai'i at Manoa. It is her wish to become a fulltime writer of children's books and poetry.

Kwajalein

You were once the pride of a canoe tradition,
a barefoot world running natural with pigs and chickens
and swimming parallel to sharks and turtles.

You were once fertile soil of sustained subsistence
– copra, fish, and coconut crabs;
and lobsters played with your children in their water games

And once you were beaches of timelessness,
host to driftwood and mutant terns –
records of hydrogeneration.

Now, distant arrows pierce your heart,
shatter your corals into cinder-block runways –
manicured lawns and golf greens.

Foreigners birdie and eagle and then ace –
a hole-in-one of missiled messages –
bullseye from snow-capped mountains of northern climes.

Can you smell the ozone hole in your sands?
The UV beams stir a tuna melt in your deceptively clear waters,
while on your knees you can only mutter, "Our Father".

The nor'westerlies howl on your shores, Kwajalein.
The garbage-illumined beaches of Ebeye –
silent and deadly.

Your ancestors' skulls dance
in the listless lolling of irradiated waves.

They say goodbye to your children
leaving for the shanty towns of Honolulu
where Big Sam keeps you forever
the Pacific beggar.

Three dogs and a bone

(the Samoan side of history – for Kilali)

It was a humid March morning in 1889,
3 dogs and 7 ships in the gurgling harbor
salivated over a bone.

They circled and sniffed and nudged;
cajoled and pulled and pushed –
must get that bone, that thick Samoan bone.

Blinded by hunger and greed
they refused to acknowledge
that other dogs already had the knuckle.

Tagaloa snickered,
Nafanua cracked her warring neck
and Jesus Christ, well, turned the other jowl.

Three together gathered a force –
a stormy, merciless force,
that made the dogs howl and whimper.

Their ships rolled and creaked, heaved and hoed –
Alas, the poor dogs were no match
for the holy trinity in their element.

Then the dogs had second thoughts
and left the bone alone –
at least for a while.

But from afar they licked and growled –
must get that bone, that thick Samoan bone.

Finally, the bone splintered –
        and the splinter became a ward of the puppy in the pack.

Horrors! cracked the rest of the bone.
What are we going to do?

The puppy yelped victory and snatched away,
hijacked the splinter to the bottom of the bay –
that coal-fuelling bay that is now pack-a-fish bay.

Today at water's edge the dog still stands
what a parent he has become
clothed in a star-spangled banner.

In his grip that breakaway splinter,
that baby bone, dancing in the water
the smelly water at the edge of the bay.

From the bottom of the bay
Splinter packs choliformed tuna –
canned gifts for the father, Chief Sam(oa).

LEMALU TATE SIMI

Lemalu Samau Tate Simi was born in Fagalii, Samoa in 1952 and educated at
Samoa College. He studied architecture/draughting in New Zealand at
Wellington Polytechnic and the Central Institute of Technology, then worked as
an architectural draughtsman at the head offices of the Ministry of Works and the
Housing Corporation in Wellington, and the Department of Public Works in
Samoa. He joined the Department of Labour, Samoa in 1978 and has been Head
of that department since 1978. His first collection of poetry, *a deeper song*, was
published in 1992, and was reprinted with the addition of new poems in 1995.
Lemalu has served as the National President of the Samoa Red Cross since 1995
and his other interests include rugby, art and music.

Two-in-one

(for John Rangihau)

I wondered
how I came to be etched
into the skin of your face
and how you came to know
the thoughts of my mind
how we both mourned

the loss of a korero
that was not ours
you, a New Zealand Maori
and I, a Samoan

Then I realised
that despite the many seas
the many hills and gullies
the many moons of time and change
that separate us
we are still one in Polynesia
united more so now than ever
in our quest for our self

Who cares?

(to the man under the Apia Town Clock Tower)

Are you a lunatic, a vagabond
that you should have the time
to loiter under the clock tower
eating leftovers and feeding
your life to the dogs?

I've seen you before
in the bus shelters of Sydney
in the pigeon parks of Wellington
drinking, sleeping, pissing
in the same clothes
on city streets

Then, I despised
the seeming purposelessness
of your existence
and your lack of value
for the invaluable
gift of life

Now, in my sorrow
I envy your solitude,
your seeming immunity
to the pain of losing
loved ones you never knew;
how you obliviously loiter

in the shadows
of the town clock tower
feeding your life to the dogs –
Who cares?

Waterfall

She had her back to me
a blanket of thick green bush
concealed her buttocks
sprawling like a wedding gown
around her thighs

I wondered what beauty
lay on the other side
of this June mirage
for I could only see her hair
of fine Chinese silver silk
cascading, melting, dissolving
into a pool at the foothills
of the Lushan mountains

*This poem was inspired by a photograph by Li Zijie of the
Jade Curtain Waterfall, Lushan Mountain, China, in a
1985 picture calendar by the China National Publishing
Industry Trading Corporation.*

NOUMEA SIMI

Noumea Simi was born at Tuasivi, Savaii, in Samoa. Educated at Samoa College
and at Massey University in New Zealand, she has served as the director of
Women's Affairs in Western Samoa. She writes in both Samoan and English, and
her first collection of poems, *Sails of Dawn*, was published in 1992.

Saipan revisited 1997

I went searching
for the legacy of six years' exile
to find the missing links of my heritage

a passing allusion in Chamorro history books
and fading memories

I was sad when they said
that all landmarks disappeared
with the pockmarked years of wars
But they knew that Tanapag

was home to the men from Samoa

I walked the beach where they landed
looking for their tracks in the pebbled sand
feeling their spirit linger
dragging their souls unwilling to the wetlands
yearning for that homeland

I could almost feel the fervour
in the heart of the man from Amoa
challenging the might of the Pacific
hoping that the rushing currents
would drive him back to his soul's destiny

I was glad that I searched
for while there is no memorial to the brave
there is in the heart of one living descendant
pride in his Samoan ancestry unyielding
to time and foreign intrusion

I was comforted to know that
all their remains made the journey home
their life in Saipan hidden in limestone
wilderness guarded by the ageless fetau
and the family of Pua; Tanapag

CAROLINE SINAVAIANA-GABBARD

Caroline Sinavaiana, Assistant Professor of English at the University of Hawai'i at Manoa, was born in 1946 on Tutuila in eastern Samoa. Her scholarly research has been supported by the Ford and Fulbright Foundations, and her international work in community-based theatre arts has been supported by the Rockefeller Foundation. Her scholarship and creative writing appear in international journals. In 2001 her collection of poetry, *Alchemies of Distance*, was published, and in 2003 her book on satirical Samoan theatre is forthcoming.

soirée

(for J. J. Wilson & Mama Day)

an alchemy of distance:
your absence, sisters, stirs longing
& embers from the muses' fire.
the spirit rises to the task, &
i from the couch/ awake now
to take up the story
where the last daughter left off/
giving voice to the silence/ inside
green mountains looming/ from a warm sea
& voice/ to the insides
of calderas/ cooled volcano's tilted cup
half-sunken to carve harbor from expanse of ocean

& witness
to the chatter of fruit-bats, sucking papaya seeds
  from their teeth in the tree outside my door
to amorous geckoes flapping splayed toes across
  window glass louvers/ out on roach patrol together?
  grabbing some gecko nookie in the odd moment?
  (but oh, i forget my manners!)
to the sound of waves soughing behind drunken guitars
  down by the store/ an occasional taxi rattling its
  hubcaps over the roadway between here & the sea.
Tutuila island, Saturday night, alone at my desk &
the party's in full swing,
ceiling fan whistling lightly/ & round
muffled barking from dogs in the next village east.

a solitude redolent of women's spiralling
talk & deepening mysteries/ your sweet voices
blaze from the pages of books/ &
the handwritten lines of letters/ our conversation
burns its winding way/ over miles of ocean &
aeons of yellow hills & rocky ledges/ that arabesque
of hearts & joined limbs of spirit.
consorts revel in the glowing quiet
of the solitary study & draw me out
again/ into the wide air/ the opening dark
to mingle w/ancestors & the scent of wild plumeria
to cut a rug in the tropical december night
to sip ginger tea/ & toast our starry confluence
across the galaxy of this moment.

death at the christmas fair: elegy for a fallen shopper

mushroom angels sprayed silver & gold,
ceramic vases like stetson hats someone sat on,
over-sized satchels for the fashionable bag lady,
and death/ stopping by next to the noodle stand/

we sit on the lava wall/ colonial amerika, late
20th century/ ketchup-dipped french fries arrested
in mid-bite/ while 2 benches away, a young cop
pounds on the dying man's chest.

sunlight plays tag w/shade & breeze, while your life
slips away/ island man/ supine on a park bench.
working man/ the soles of your feet/ bare brown & muscle
thick/ jump w/each slam of the fist to your waning heart.

the breath punched suddenly out of us too/
swallowing silence w/our diet cokes,
we speak of our own fathers dying young,
of men as a fragile breed, endangered somehow.

mouth of the afternoon closes suddenly
stilled/ your spirit taking its leave
in a sunny moment, while crowds shop
the largesse of amerika: kitsch, knick-knacks,

bric-a-brac & over-priced t-shirt dresses
dried grasses in garish colors/ gaily
beribboned clumps of pathos/ fake tapa
& hawaiian deities air-brushed on tanks & tees.

maybe you died of disgust, uncle/
the sight of all this expensively crafted trash:
decorator throw pillows in slick island motifs/
the colors of vomit.

i don't blame you, uncle; nothing you could afford here
anyway. maybe you died of shame/ consumptive
amerika grasping/ hawaiian land desecrated w/plastic
commodities, lacy dresses for other people's daughters,

trendy earrings for other men's wives.
"this makes me so sick, i could die,"
you might have thought. & so you did
or might have done.

leaving a small girl crying & the cops
walking their somber faces away
& me standing at the bamboo sculptures booth
between tibetan-style jackets & koa-backed clocks/

my only salute to your passing: a slow dirge
on bamboo rain stick/ way outta *my* price range/
a shopper's farewell: the sound of rain
moving from manoa valley to the sea

in your honor/ i leave the park/
hands empty, shopping bag empty/
like you, uncle/
i protest.

Sā Nafanuā

(for my sisters)

high-stepping in pink
patent leather boots
arms linked, we march together
in raggedy-assed lines, holes in our
sequined stockings/ crooked at the seams
under rainbow-colored tights and feather
cloaks/ this band of warriors/ your
frisky daughters, my dear/
at your service/ our weapons slung
across shoulder & hip/ paintbrush & camera
laptop & lawbook/ your freckled daughters/
after-jets burning away illusion/ attachment/
clearing the channel for the birth
of ourselves & each other/ your
gypsy daughters.

we move down to the sea;
our sons carry the boat
bringing coconut, breadfruit,
taro and papaya to plant the new land.
babies chortle at the breast
the bigger ones chasing sandcrabs
back into their holes/ our brothers
hoist the sails & festoon us
w/maile garlands/ pua & 'awapui
flower-scented aura of our people/
protect us mother/ we follow your
ocean patch to the world above
the dark cave/ guide us mother
the sea serpent lurks beneath waves
monster ego/ demons gnaw on the rigging
steady us mother/ your eye lights the way
your heart moves our blood
your hand steers our boat
and plants us like seeds in the new
land/ sing for us tinā.

MUA STRICKSON-PUA

A New Zealand-born Samoan, Mua Strickson-Pua is of the aiga Pue of Papa Sataua and the aiga Purcell of Malaela. He is also known as Rev. MC, and describes himself as, among other things, a poet, artist, co-founder of Street Poets Black, comedian, storyteller, social commentator, chaplain and community worker. He is currently celebrating 20 years as a performing Pasifikan poet, and his work incorporates strong themes of being a New Zealand-born Pasifikan, of cultural and social change, faith challenges and the use of Pasifika Hip Hop poetry for healing and therapy.

Oh Samoan Boy

Oh Samoan boy.
Who will lament your deeds?

They say you killed a palagi taxi driver.
Stop press headlines.
Descriptions like cowardly deeds.
Savage, brutal, unprovoked attack on an
innocent bystander, a worthy member of
the community, a family man.
Who will look after his family now?
Work mates giving testimony
to what a nice bloke he was.
While commenting on the dangers
of their job.
The police praised for apprehending
such an animal.
Once again the welfare state chalked up
another success story.
Justice system swift and impartial
creaking machinery now jolted into action
with public fervour emotions swelled.
Justice must be seen to be done.
Social critics descended with their commentary
like vultures picking at the last remains
of those human bones.

He was a Samoan.
A boy of 15 years.
School dropout.
Unemployed.
A gang member.

He had a social worker.
He had a probation officer.
He also visited Social Welfare,
Labour, and Justice Department.

Now he killed someone now somebody.

Police finally found him.
Court put him in Mt Eden prison.
Psychiatric assessment carried out.
High Court served its sentence on murder.

His mother cried openly at court.
While the press had a field day.
Father sat in quiet solitude.
With his faraway look to home.
They were aware of their shame.

Feeling naked before righteous eyes.
All those old feelings flooding back.
When they first came to this land.
This feeling of being different.
Now parents of a murderer.

Once again they felt left out.
Not being in control of their destiny.
Yet no matter how hard they worked
it did not seem to make a difference.
Over years an acceptance of this state
silently sets in.

Oh Samoan boy.
When they passed judgment.
In that dock with your Sunday best.
Your gaze cut right through us
in that courtroom on that day.
It was as if everything around you
ceased to exist.

You all alone.
Body staunch.
Yet mechanical movements.
Dull by emotions escaping.
Your spirit to live had died.

So serve your sentence.
Locked away to protect society.
Or out of sight out of mind.
Meaning we don't want to be
reminded of our failures.

Oh Samoan boy.
Who will lament your deeds?

J. C. STURM

J. C. Sturm was born in Opunake, New Zealand and her tribal affiliations are to
Taranaki iwi and Whakatōhea. She has published poetry and short stories in
periodicals and anthologies since 1947. Her first collection of short stories, *The
House of the Talking Cat*, was published in 1983. Her first collection of poems,
Dedications, was published in 1996 and received the Honour Award for poetry in
the 1997 Montana New Zealand Book Awards. Her second collection of poems
was published in 2000. She worked as a librarian in Wellington for 23 years and
retired to Paekākāriki where she still lives.

After the Brodsky Quartet

She listens with lowered head
To its singing beneath her bow,
Holds firmly with velvet knees
Its glowing symmetry,
Then movingly reveals
An unsuspected passion;

Later, in a small dark room,
Turns to her waking husband's
Urgent touch, and after,
Beside his heavy sleeping,
Dreams of that other lover
Singing in her private space.

History lesson

Believe me when I tell you
With no introduction,
In spite of its beauty
The planet is an urupā.

Don't be dismayed.
Out of its concrete graves
Children grow like grass
Perpetuating us.

No language, certainly not
Yours or mine, can tell them
Anything not entered
Already in their genes.

If we are not too clever,
Some of us might help
Some of them access
The programme, nothing more.

All of us straddle
Fault lines of meaning
Waiting for the Big One
To open them up.

Meanwhile observe these dancers,
How perfectly and full of grace
They repeat themselves.
Shiva knew a thing or two

About Being. He could be
My ancestor's cousin
And yours. We share the same
Whakapapa,

Same geology too.
What is more, there is nothing
That has not been before,
The new repeats the old.

We are simply variations
On original themes.
Why are you dismayed?
We carry history in our genes

Like messages in bottles.
Surely that is enough.
Don't tell me you believe,
You want, more than this.

What, in God's name, what?

New Year's Eve 1998

acknowledgements to J.K.B.

Fifty years later, the brilliance
Of that Rocket Show
On an Otago beach
Has faded. Now ordinary
Starlight must be enough
To travel by.

Maybe next century,
That is to say, quite soon,
An unexpected comet
Will set the sky on fire
Like that infamous
Mushroom-spawning flash;

Or simply transmute us
Into heavenly bodies
With no (not likely)
Flashy fireworks. But now
Enjoy being ordinary:
Eating, sleeping, making love.

Tomorrow we might go
Swimming, weather permitting.

At times I grieve

At times I grieve for you
Knowing one day you are bound
To grieve for me.
How will you be after the shock
And after shocks of my going,
When you have done what must be
Done and put me in the hole
With some small ceremony?

Be warned; my absence
In the empty house
Will hit you like a fist,
Emptiness fill you
To overflowing, silence
Wail my name in your ears,
And all the precious, useless
Things I had to leave behind
Weigh your hearts down
Like lumps of lead.

Go home; eat, drink, be
As merry as you can,
Make love as though
For the very last time
Warming each other through
And through to the still centre,
Then in the quiet that follows
After, learn how quickly,
How easily, love makes
Everything possible again.

Man talk, woman talk

All cocks and cunts
are basically the same,
he told her.
Size and age
don't matter much,
it's what you do
with what you've got
that counts.

All hearts and minds
are basically the same,
she told him.
Aches and breaks
don't matter much,
it's what you do
in spite of them
that counts.

And then they carried on
like nothing had been said.

Tangi

Think of the many dead, you
Who would lie with your dead
In the whare nui
Beneath the kōwhaiwhai
Before the tukutuku
Below the tupuna
Who watch over
All who lie here,
The living and the dead.

Think of him who lies
Beside you, separate now.
Mihi to him
He is lonely,
Tangi for him
He does not want to go.
Tangi for those
Who tangi for him.
Tangi with those
Who tangi for you.
Mihi and tangi
Will bind you,
Bind you together.

Remember your dead:
The very young
Taken so soon,
The strong axed down
In their pride,
The very old

Who simply slipped away.
Mihi to them
Tangi for them
Be bound with them.

Imagine those before
The ones before
The ones you knew.
Think and imagine:
How it was for them,
So it will be
The same for you.
Tangi for them
Tangi for you
Lie there, lie there
Bound with the living
And your dead.

He waiata tēnei mō Parihaka

Have you heard of Parihaka
Between
Maunga Taranaki
And the sea

Where Te Whiti o Rongomai
And Tohu Kakahi
Preached
Passive resistance, not war?

Have you heard of Parihaka
Where Taranaki iwi
Gathered
Seeking a way to keep their land?

Non-violence was their choice
Peace their aim
Raukura their badge
Ploughs their only weapons.

They pulled down fences
Pulled out pegs
Then ploughed whatever
The settlers claimed was theirs.

Have you heard of Parihaka's
Boys and girls
Waiting outside the gates
When the mounted soldiers came

To rape and murder
Pillage and burn
To take Te Whiti and Tohu away
With all the ploughmen

And ship them south
To build a causeway
Around Dunedin's
Wintry harbour?

Have you heard of Taranaki iwi
Denied a trial,
Chained like dogs
In sealed caves and tunnels?

Ngāi Tahu smuggled
Food and blankets
To the prisoners
Comforted the sick in the dark.

Kua ngaro ngā tangata
Kua ngaro i te pō!
Auē te mamae
That followed after!

If you haven't heard of Parihaka,
Be sure
Your grandchildren will
And their children after them,

History will see to that.
But for now,
He waiata tēnei mō Parihaka –
Auē, auē, a-u-ē –

At the Museum on Puke-ahu

He waiata mō ngā taonga

It was too special an occasion
For anonymity.

Nothing less
Than a public show of origin and identity
Belonging and commitment
Would do
For the job to be done:
The lifting of a tapu
The launching of a new taonga
Ngā Tangata Taumata Rau
Into the world of books

With
Karakia
Haka
Whaikōrero
Waiata.

The tohunga led
The tangata whenua
Kaumatua
Manuhiri
From foyer to echoing hall
Pakeha present to Maori past
One kind of knowing and feeling
To another way of being.

We laid down
Our personal taonga
Of individuality
As koha on the marae
And made the perilous passage
From one world to another
Diminished and dependent
On a strength
Other than our own

Becoming no more than
A likeness to a faded photo
The bearer of another's name
The end of a line
On a whakapapa
A mark on a page
A notch on a stick
A mere speck
Of historical dust.

Our shadows on
The polished floor
Kept us company
Like secret allies
As we moved toward
The whare whakairo
Te Hau-ki-Turanga
In the great hall
Where Tāwhirimātea
Shattered the air
Around the high dome
Above us

And all the old taonga
Moved restlessly
In their glass-caged sleep
Dreaming of their prime
Of release and being
Taken home –
     "Awhinatia mai
      Arohatia ra" –
Sharing with us
The painful truth
Of irretrievable loss.

Splitting the Stone

for John

You brought back
Carefully, nervously
A heavy grey boulder
From that other beach
Up north –
The place I call home
When I feel inclined –
A narrow iron strip
Between land and sea
With several old battlefields
Close by
And a guardian mountain.

On a clear day
If you are lucky
And really quick
You may see him
Even from here,
A small opal cone
On a blue horizon
Northwest of Kapiti.

And then
As I had dreamed
The night before
You started to make
According to instructions,
A flax pounder
Like the Old Ones
Used to use
(Some can still be found
With other missing things
In various museums)

Striking stone on stone
Carefully, patiently
While I kept away
As I knew I should
Waiting for the stone to split
As I knew it would
And let the Mauri through.

And after
Your amazed silence,
I watched you set to
Forgetting the pounder
And all those
Sad museum pieces,
And make instead
Like the Old Ones used to,
A stone dwelling
For the newcomer –
A place to call home
When he feels inclined –

Carving it steel on stone
Carefully, lovingly
In his image

So the world will know
It is meant for him
And him only.

And when it was finished
You stood there
In the small space between
The roses and the taupata,
Heavy grey rain
Soaking through your clothes
And the pores of your skin,
And looked in wonder
At what you had done,
Nursing a bruised hand.

ROBERT SULLIVAN

Robert Sullivan (Ngāpuhi/Irish) was born in 1967. He has published four books of
poetry, *Jazz Waiata* (AUP, 1990), *Piki Ake!* (AUP, 1993), *Star Waka* (AUP, 1999) and
Captain Cook in the Underworld (AUP, 2002), as well as a graphic novel, *Maui:
Legends of the Outcast* (Godwit, 1996). *Weaving Earth and Sky*, a retelling of Maori
myths and legends, was published in 2002. *Jazz Waiata* won the PEN Award for
Best First Book of Poetry and *Star Waka* was shortlisted in the Poetry section of the
2000 Montana New Zealand Book Awards. Robert has co-edited, with Reina
Whaitiri, a contemporary Maori literature issue of the American journal *Manoa*
and also co-edits the online literary journal *Trout*. Robert lives in Auckland and is
the Maori Services Manager at the University of Auckland Library.

Māui Tosses the Hook

Tangaroa
make your sea lie smooth
            as greenstone
aid the flight of my bone
gentle your friend the summer wind
so he casts like whakapapa
from the mouths of tohunga
                make the line taut

the hook unyielding
    pull it on
    pull it strong
make Te-Ika-a-Māui come!

I walked over the hill

Pockets of totara forest reclaim what few remains there are
of the Karetu pā. Young black ferns protect crumbling earth,

ponga roots exposed where ponga walls once rose, but no more
room for sentiment. It's a chief's eye view of the valley too –

the river at hills' feet glides, in repose, by the old metal
that brought you here, took us home so often. September

the second, a softer season, brings teatree blossoms, scatters
wasps, bees loud as fire engines, sends adrenalin through me

as if I were a fireman. Over the hill Nanna Bella shows me
orchids, warms goat milk in a microwave oven, lets me feed

the bleaters. "Wash your hands when you leave the pā."
I observe the ritual of bread too. It is no man's hill.

Waka 62. A narrator's note

There is no Odysseus to lead this fleet –
not even Māui who sent waka to their petrification,

the waka Mahunui, for instance, placed exactly
in the centre of the South Island at Māui's command.

I have only waka floating beneath the stars,
at night and in the day, directed by swells,

whose crews are sustained not by seabirds
or fish, but by memory – some in conflict

with the written record. I have only seen waka at rest.
They are beings worthy of the company they keep –

tohunga to furnish voyagers with karakia, taniwha for security,
the very stars in motion with them.

I cannot provide you with a leader of the fleet.
This fleet navigated centuries. The names

of captains were known to their colleagues
as ancestors. The Pacific was a far-flung society

– waka, cocooned in Aotearoa,
stopped returning to Hawaiki, dropped their sails,

clambered overland into rivers, burrowed
into mountains, reefs, flew into words

sung at tangi, polished speeches,
seen by the pāua eyes of gods and ancestors

whose real eyes, blinking in the light
of their lives millennia and centuries ago,

saw the vehicles themselves –
spacecraft, oxygen tanks, caravans led by elephants,

vehicles of concept, exploration, sails a vortex
ribbed by people shouting names down into the Great Sea.

Waka 76

Tangaroa slams his pint on the bar,
"gissa nother," he hisses – the bartender jumps,
slides a frothy wave the length of the bay –
the crowd of furseals resume their conversations,
slapping each other on the backs.

A guy with a waka attitude walks in,
leans over looking at Tangaroa –
"I'll have what the wet guy's having
since he's gonna pay for it."
The fur seals fly in all directions.

Tangaroa looks him up and down,
checks out his moko and his waka.
"You're one of Tane's kids ain't ya.
That means we're kin!"
He pays for the drink.

Waka 99

If waka could be resurrected
they wouldn't just come out
from museum doors smashing
glass cases revolving and sliding
doors on their exit

they wouldn't just come out
of mountains as if liquified
from a frozen state
the resurrection wouldn't just
come about this way

the South Island turned to wood
waiting for the giant crew
of Māui and his brothers
bailers and anchors turned back
to what they were when they were strewn

about the country by Kupe
and his relations
the resurrection would happen
in the blood of the men and women
the boys and girls

who are blood relations
of the crews whose veins
touch the veins who touched the veins
of those who touched the veins
who touched the veins

who touched the veins
of the men and women from the time
of Kupe and before.
The resurrection will come
out of their blood.

Waka 100

Stroke past line 1642 into European time.
Stroke past 1769 and the introduction of the West

Stroke on the approach to 1835
and formal Northern Maori sovereignty.

Stroke into the New World and stop.

Crews alight, consign waka
to memory, family trees, remove the prowed
tauihu, drape the feathered mana
around the whare-womb
of the next crew

who are to remember waka into the beginning
of centuries years minutes hours seconds
long and short hands centred on Greenwich

each person
of waka memory to hold their thoughts,
each person of seagoing
and waterborn descent whose hard waka
are taken away.

And years later,
we ask our ancestors to wake,
whose mokopuna are carving in eyes,
restoring chiselled features, mouths
coming out of wood, genitals, feet planted
on shoulders winding into stars on ceilings,
our ancestors of a culture that has held
its breath through the age of Dominion.
They've adzed waka out for them –
the memories, intricate knowledge,
fleet leaders, their reasons for being –
shoulders that carried so many waka –
summoning souls of myriads of names
above hundreds of waka names.

And you waka, who have seen heaven,
the guts of the ocean, brought terror and pleasure,
who have exhausted your crews of home thoughts
who have lifted songs above the waves
of the greatest and deepest ocean,
rise – rise into the air – rise to the breath –

rise above valleys into light and recognition –
rise where all who have risen sing your names.

And you, Urizen, Jupiter, Io Matua Kore,
holder of the compasses – wind compass,
solar compass, compass encompassing known
currents, breather of the first breath
in every breathing creature,
guide the waka between islands,
between years and eyes of the Pacific
out of mythologies to consciousness.

And you stars, the ancestors,
nuclear orbs, red giants, white dwarves,
burn brilliantly, burn on the waka down there,
burn on waka riding valleys,
burn on waka on mountain summits,
burn on waka in the night,
burn on waka past the end of the light.

CHRIS TAMAIPAREA

Chris Tamaiparea is of Tūwharetoa/Ngāti Whātua descent. He was born in the
Auckland suburb of Glen Innes, the great suburb where glue sniffing was
invented. Residing in the United Kingdom, he has never given up his dream of
opening the batting for the New Zealand cricket team. His long-suffering partner
Donnelle believes this will never happen.

coast triptych

(to be arranged in any order)

!
moana puts on a show
a sea of blue kites
leashed to the sky
by three strands
of early sunlight

@
sea breeze pianissimo
we two share
secret conversations
the dusty ears of a
pohutukawa
are burning
its bough leans
my way

#
one opportunist leaf
traces a path
a small net in the air
trying to catch
the ocean breathing

VII

and when after seven months three women and much
thought you kissed me on the lips and not
the cheek as we had been doing
cordially i became highly
irritated and could
not wipe the grin
off my face

another poem about trees

a friend of mine said
that ken mair said
that at the mention of the word
green
pakeha kids think of traffic lights and
maori kids think of trees

apparently mister mair
is a really radical type
but no one i know
has ever stepped
on the gas
when they saw
a tree

a cartoon

megan is a waif
the mass of her hair
is physical *kinetics*
a huge bobbing dreadlocked
blonde convulsion of an affair
sitting
a yellow tarantula upon her shoulders
paint her hair green
remove her clothes
hey presto!
a blade of silverbeet!

TRACEY TAWHIAO

Tracey Tawhiao of Ngaiterangi and Tūwharetoa has a BA LLB from the
University of Auckland. She spends a lot of time doing work for her tribal trust.
Tracey began writing poetry five years ago and for two years performed her
poetry before stopping to reflect and to write a novel. With her husband, she is
travelling in France to promote a Polynesian hip-hop music label and bring
Polynesian music to the world.

Why Am I Auditioning for TV?

Do you watch TV the director asked, pointing her Hi8 in my face
No I don't to tell the truth I don't know who has the time to watch
No time during the day, it's just crap on anyway
All that shit those Americans go on about all day along
That her husband slept with her sister and her brother
Or Oprah drooling over some stars in that familiar way
Days of our Lives should be called No Lives
the whole medium is about money, you know, advertising
or just bad it tells about the fucked up lives of Americans
And now TV4 thinks we want to watch our own fucked up lives
The New Zealand content is so important to identity they say
And then they show us who we are and I recognise no one
Because this is not reality, it is a distortion of reality, creating a new one

So I see a girl who looks like me but then her thoughts belong to Barbie
There are never the things which make life interesting
Like Maori radicals crashed out on your floor snoring hard
Like the newslady smoking a roach off the end of a matchstick
Like a shot of a McCahon in a dirty hole in the ground
Maybe TV would be worth a look if it didn't want
To sell me soap I don't need and Tampax I can't use
It's trying too hard to tell me that I'm white and that I must consume
That I need to be thin and straight that my leaders are con men
Even if they are con men I didn't say they were my leaders the TV did
Having said my piece to this director it seems I'm not quite right for the job.

Maori Girl

She can't get a job but she's used to that
Most of her family can't get jobs either
The man next door says she doesn't want one
A pretty girl like you must get all kinds of offers
She isn't sure why but he gives her the creeps

Last week she had an interview at Shanton's
She had had to borrow Mary's good dress
Mary said it looked too big but what else could she do
The lady at Shanton's was too busy to see
What a great shop assistant she would be

The man next door said she looked good
He asked her over for a cup of tea, she said yes
No one had ever asked her over for a cup of tea before
He talked non stop about himself as she drank the tea
He said she was too pretty to be a Maori

When she said she had to go he asked her why
She told him she had to look after her sister's kids
He told her she should get herself a real job
She left but wondered about that word real
Her sister's kids were pretty real she thought

The lady from Shanton's called back the news was bad
She was too shy the woman said, to be a sales person
That she needed to get over being shy, get confident
Get confident, real job, too pretty to be a Maori
She knew the dress had been too big but what were her choices

While she was watching her sister's kids, she cried
Why did that man make her feel bad why did he say,
Being a Maori didn't exactly get you anywhere in life
She had to stop crying because the baby was crying
She picked her up and kissed and held her tight

She closed her eyes she hummed a song, she rocked from side to side.

The Phantom of the Maori

This is rude I know but why is the Aotea Centre packed
one hundred dollars a seat for this mindless toss about
an ugly man who wants a beautiful woman to sing for him
He's named the Phantom of the Opera, she's supposed to care
He tells her to tap into her dark side so she will think he's OK
This guy is dreaming, that mask just covers a pitiful egomaniac

We couldn't stay not even for the quality of the set design
We had to leave before I fell asleep, or worse before I stood up
To shout at the audience for dressing up and buying into this shit
Wondered what we could create with the budget of this thing
The thought of something about our gods had me lost in the magnificent sets
And the divine dialogue of my forebears
And if they thought this was a musical they'd be so overawed by our waiata
This thought was only just processed before I started to think cynically

About the scraps over which iwi had more rights to the story
Who owns the waiata and why we can't refer to Maui
There'd be endless hui to discuss whether to share this sacred history
Then we'd have to bless the sets each night, a budget for the tohunga
Maybe that's a better story, the one about the dispossession of mana
How it turns the concept of Maori into something a budget can cater for
How it has the capacity to make a Maori say and do things for the money
And then I think that's what happens when you don't have any money, and your
value system's undermined and your culture denigrated and no longer do
your beliefs command any respect

When you watch the reverence those with money receive
You might just want some for the wrong reasons
You might just say something is Maori to get a piece of the action
You might just do what's been done to you and shit on someone else

I started with the Phantom of the Opera but the interesting thing of course is the
   phantom of the Maori.

Weaving

I read my poems to my cousin while she weaves
She's cutting bits off this way and that, all is well
Nothing fogs her strong hands as they move in and out
I wish my poems had her delivery, maybe I'll cut bits too
Maybe I'll cut every bloody bit, what will this leave?
A string of self-indulgent angst, can't sell that shit
All my cousin's cutting has a destination, a point
She collects up all the scraps and makes them into a thing
What should I do with all my leftovers aye, chuck them in the bin?

What the hell do I think I'm doing with these words I ask her
Wish I could do something useful, weaving words is hopeless
Weaving harakeke is a gift from the gods and you can make a living
All I can do is make something from inside my curly woolly head
Sometimes I wonder why I hang myself out there, nerves bent
Finding out the truth of the things inside, outside my head
Don't worry she says in her calm and weaving way
Just go out there and tell the world *your* words in *your* own way
My cousin of course always always has just the right thing to say.

McCahon

Yesterday when I was at the shop
A man, a complete stranger came up to me
And said – you bastards stole that McCahon
I said fuck off I'm busy
He started to pull my trolley
You bastards stole that McCahon
I tried to push past him with my trolley
I started to feel mad
Yeah arsehole I stole it
Colin came to me in a vision
He said girl I don't like how DOC treat Maori
He said steal it and just remember, use a yellow car
This is not a joke you stupid bitch
Excuse me, who are you calling stupid bitch, arsehole
I know you fullas took it
For your political whatsitcalled
Movement, and can you please create some movement away from me

I saw you with that tattooed faced fulla
You lot should go back to where you came from
Excuse me arsehole, we were here when you arrived
And what would a redneck like you know about
Art, Maori or political movements
With that I pushed my trolley really hard
He stumbled a bit and that's when I kicked him
He fell into a potplant display
I walked as fast as I could and I never looked back.

A Lawyer and a Builder

My uncle drives out to my house with his mate a builder
They talk in builder talk where a variety of grunts has meaning
I wonder whether I should do the girl thing and make a cuppa tea
Instead I dare to be unlike what they were expecting and grunt too
They look a bit confused but I think they are just confused by my feminine accent
I try to get a grunt out with more resonance, more depth
Now they really are beginning to take a second look at me
I decide to talk in my own housewife-don't-mess-with-me voice
"I really want to get rid of those aluminium windows, I want wooden ones"
If my uncle's mate didn't understand grunts, he understands this less
"Why you want to get rid of those for, you have to paint the wood ones every five
    years"
He shakes his head and looks suspiciously at my uncle, who looks away
We move into another room for his inspection, no cuppa tea closer
This looks good says the builder in animated tones, no grunting at all
I imitate my uncle's no nonsense voice this time, anything for a kick, I am a housewife
I want all that concrete exposed and that ceiling replaced, that wall out but then I smile
    pleasantly
The grunting starts again, they don't want me to understand
My uncle takes his mate outside and I hear him say
I told you she was different, she can't just have any old builder
She needs someone who won't talk down to her, who won't mind her being odd
She's always been different this one, my uncle looks over to me
She might not sound altogether but she's a lawyer, yeah man she is
They both look at me so I smile and say, Cuppa tea, I'll just put the jug on.

APIRANA TAYLOR

Born in New Zealand, Apirana Taylor is of Ngāti Porou, Te Whānau a Apanui, Ngā Puhi, Ngāti Ruanui and Ngāti Pākehā descent. He is a poet, novelist, short-story writer, playwright, actor and painter, who tries to earn a living as a freelance artist, but currently teaches creative writing at Whitireia Polytechnic. Apirana has won awards for his poetry and drama and is currently working on a manuscript of two of his plays to be published by the Pohutukawa Press. His publications include three books of poetry, *Eyes of the Ruru*, *Three Shades* and *Soft Leaf Falls of the Moon*, two books of short stories, *He Rau Aroha* and *Ki Te Ao*, and one novel, *He Tangi Aroha*. He has been the writer in residence at Massey University and Canterbury University, and he has toured Europe reading his poetry, which has also been translated into German.

soft leaf falls of light

Soft leaf falls of light

soft light falls of leaf

leaf soft light falls

light soft leaf falls

light falls leaf soft

ligth light light

soft leaf falls of light

Whakapapa

For too long now he'd sought his whakapapa
sought and unfound whakapapa
whirled in the wind
whistled in the leaves
first there was Rangi and Papa
that was the first whakapapa
or was the Te Kore
then there was dark and light
night and day
what was that whakapapa
and all the different kinds of dark and light
the light turning the world turning
the night the long night
whakapapa whakapapa
who was he, he began again
the moko on the chief's face
or those strong enough to take it is whakapapa
the mauri, eternal life force
tihei, that's the sneeze
tihei tihei tihei
whakapapa whakapapa
ties you to the land
the ropes are cut
what did he inherit
dole queues longer than your arm
uneducated unmotivated unqualified, drunk again
of neither this world nor the other
so Rangi the skyfather and Papatūānuku the earthmother
lay together in love's embrace
the Gods were born
and then remember Māui
Māui Māui Māui and Tāwhaki climbing the vine
and the marae
whakapiri tonu whakapiri tonu
there is more much more
lift yourself up boy
where the flowers grow is the whakapapa of light
where the flowers sleep is the whakapapa of darkness
you are Ngāti
this is your inheritance
the sky and earth and all that lies between

Te Ihi

From where does it come, te hā
the life breath
and what strange winds blow
through this house
in the drift and flow
of whaikōrero
the call
ka ea ka ea
it is clear, it is clear
whakapiri tonu whakapiri tonu
hold fast, hold fast to what
te ihi, te ihi, te ihi
te ihi, what is that
te ihi, what is this word
te ihi, te ihi, what is it
kia mau, kia mau ki te aha
he pāua mura ahi ngā kanohi o Tumatauenga
the flashing eyes of Tū
haka it is haka
lightning flashing in the sky
rapa rapa te uira
ka tangi te whatitiri
and thunder
the beat of the feet till the earth shakes
kia whakatahoki au i a au
from where does it come, te hā
the life breath, te ihi
the sobbing wailing and laughter

The Fale

(To my friend Iosefa)

The fale I think
is a beautiful house
because it's cool
you can sit there
and talk
and let the wind
wash over you
and cool you
you can see the stars
and night sky

I like that
because in my world
the wind talks
the river talks
the tribes of rocks and stones talk
because they are people
and the stars sing karakia

In the fale
I can breathe and communicate
because it's a house
without walls
and I sit here
drinking Vailima
learning about Samoa
and listening
to my mate Iosefa

In Samoa at Solaua Fatumanava

(To Momoe and family)

Spun out
in the modern fast food
take away world
of computer jets
and instant everything

I am ever restless
in search of change
continual revolution
my friends Momoe and Stephan
take me to the centre of their island
the pito of the Universe
the umbilical cord
the earth's belly button
a volcanic plateau
where I lie like the rocks
scattered by a giant's hand
in the cool flowing mountain water
where the spiders argue
with the wind
who talks to the trees
who sing
about the rain
who gave himself
to the river again
who let himself
splash free over the rocks
back to the web
by the river
where the spider
gave up weaving the air
and ran back
to his house
and busily bounced up
and down
on his trampoline
they've been doing this
for fifty million years now
they see no reason for change
at Fatumanava
the centre of the universe
and for a tiny moment
in time
neither do I

ALICE TE PUNGA SOMERVILLE

Born in Wellington, Aotearoa/New Zealand, in 1975, with affiliations to
Te Atiawa, Alice grew up in the Auckland suburb of Glen Innes. She has a BA in
English and History, and an MA (with 1st class honours) in English, both from the
University of Auckland. With the help of a Fulbright scholarship, she is currently
at Cornell University (in Ithaca, NY, USA), completing a PhD in English, with a
minor in American Indian studies. Her publications include a chapter on
Maori/Pakeha mixed race writing in *Mixed Race Literature* (ed. J. Brennan,
Stanford University Press, 2002) and *Nga Take Atawhai*, a report on the provision of
earning support to Maori students (published by the Student Learning Centre,
Massey University Albany, 1999).

dishevel (a verb)

miss six has had a haircut and lost a tooth
master four has a pencil and needs a sharpener
master just-three has got a big gob of tomato sauce on his lip
baby has been growing hair and it looks like it might have curls

Dad left in the weekend. He won't be back.

Mum's crying, and it's chips for tea again
and she doesn't care if they drink some of her coke.

You're peering into my face

My cousin Rachel
has a Maori nose
she's got Chinese eyes
the ash blonde hair of an Illinois German.

When you conduct these border controls
I wish I too could show a face
that you'd see
and accept as my whakapapa passport.

Whose Home?

You will not take my grandfather
To eat at your table;
Will not usher him in at your door,
Smile,
Chatter,
Offer him treats.
You won't fuss, making sure the potatoes mash,
The meat cooks
The cake cools.
You will not pull out his chair
Serve pepper
Serve salt
Watermelon won't be sliced,
Wine unopened,
Beer unpoured.

You will not take him, will not invite him,
Will not wave as he leaves.

Because his home is here.
His heart is wide.
His skin is dark.

Mauri

A round white wreath
tied with a silver cord
hangs in front of my window.
Most people who know me well
still haven't seen it there
even though it's been in my every home.

My mother made it for me
while I read Alice Walker
and my aunty tried to die.
Her last breaths are held in my wreath:
they rustle the white fabric
and make it tap against the open window frame.

I guess you could say
it's just the wind that makes it move
I guess I could say that too.

But my spirit wouldn't agree
because it hears her still,
whispering to me.

KONAI HELU THAMAN

Born and raised in Tonga, Konai Helu Thaman was educated both there and in New Zealand, where she gained her BA in geography at the University of Auckland and completed teacher training at Auckland Secondary Teachers' College. She taught high school in Tonga before going to the USA for further study; she gained her MA in International Education from the University of California in Santa Barbara in 1974. She joined the University of the South Pacific in the same year as a lecturer in geography and sociology, was awarded a PhD by that institution in 1988, and has been there ever since. She currently holds a Personal Chair in Pacific Education and Culture and a UNESCO Chair in Teacher Education and Culture. Konai has published five collections of poetry: *You, the Choice of My Parents* (1974), *Langakali* (1981), *Hingano* (1987), *Kakala* (1993) and *Songs of Love* (1999), had one collection translated into German (Inselfur, 1987) and her work is studied in schools throughout the Pacific. Konai is married with two adult children.

Readers and Writers

today wellington wakes
to strikes and sex
education
flood damage
royal avalanches
and the state sector bill

i wake to the sound
of wind and water
heralding the arrival of kupe
kumara and con men
(but there is no one to be conned)

i wonder what he would see
perhaps a tree
with too many broken branches

Living among the trees

(for Randy, '89)

nineteen years
is a long time
by today's standards
perhaps the ground
made it possible to live
among the trees

lives lived under
clear skies defy
the flavour of storms
you're not alone
if you looked in or up
through the canopies
of silent songs

these last wounded weeks
have moved rather sluggishly
and as rain descended slowly
among plants insisting on growing
i can see you clearly
holding out your hand

Heilala

heilala
we've waited far too long
for you to move within us
give us strength to see the scars
of those who went before us
when things did seem entirely wrong
like people born and buried
believing they'd been left alone
to bleed instead of bargaining

when long ago you came
a stranger kept apart
by distance too remote
for us to win and guard

at times your face seemed close
arriving unannounced
we knew we had no choice
but load the raft and start

we left for many places
we entered eyes still closed
yet we could feel the fragrance
a power touching those
who craved instead to ride the waves
towards the blowholes not the shore
then prayed to maui for his mana
to mend their broken oar

now it's time to move again
towards those islands far beyond
the capacity of words to name
and nurture all year long
we let our words prise open
hidden caverns of the dawn
and break the sullen solitude
of a sea once unknown

for we cannot let illiteracy
again keep us apart
mortgage our identity
or even sell our pride
we do not want to suffer pain
privately at the end
because we know deep inside
we've only ourselves to blame

Kakala Folau

(a gift of love)

take this kakala my friend
kulukona langakali heilala
symbols of times
when love and life
were one

when the fragrance of falahola
embraced strangers to our shores
forests of mapa and hehea
sang songs of celebration
while ahi and vunga consoled
friends parting

but we were young then
trembling at the rhythm
of trees
that kept our secrets
from falling and spilling
over stones and sea

wondering
if the salted winds sweeping
slowly across the eyes
of the siale tafa
would whisper our thoughts
into the heart of the huni tree

Weekend in Auckland

a weekend in auckland
is good
for discovering again
old meeting places
in the park
hoping they have stories
to tell about the adventures
of a once youthful time

down under the magnolia trees
the bench which took the weight
of our first kiss
is still there
the fountain continues to beat
like an artificial heart
and the flowers continue to die
with each passing day

and there hovering high above
is the tower clock
now dwarfed by the reality
of its own time
its striking shadow a reminder
that the heart's best defence
at this time
is forgetting

Another Dimension

(for the caretaker)

you're early, he said
you new?
yes, i said, watching
the heavy keys
which locked and unlocked
our knowing
that we have met before
in some other dimension

i remember
those dreamlike days
at waipu district high
the church soaring
above the graveyard
(there are always graves
near churches in new zealand)

the night passing of people
unaware of prayers for progress
to slow down
the wind wailing
through the cabbage trees
the rain rumbling
drowning first-time tears

i remember banks of gorse
the familiar fragrance of flowing water
carving pathways across the brynderwyn hills
the eerie silence
of people in buses
forcing their way across the placid plains

that nurtured now part-time farmers
i remember discovering rain once more
flowing down the land
and he unlocking the door
splitting open my world
letting me into another frontier
where the soothing silence
of his garden cooled
my homesick fears

only today i realise
i had made contact
with the earth

Hingano

yesterday the rain
crushed the fragrance
of the hingano
and love dust wept
quietly on the petals
heavy
awkwardly pleading
with the wind

you came
and closed the door
on my face
suffocating the moment
in the bitter air
and slowly the weight of words
settled down into
the irrational length
of the night

today
the early morning sun saw
the thorns
in the thicket tract
and slowly its healing heat
cut gentle rings of light
on the shimmering sorrow
of the hingano

You and Me

i do not want to catch
your ball of sand
you and i and
the kingfisher
only watch trivial spirits

chance came out of nowhere
slashed and burned the ground
the harvest was good
a story awakes in your eyes
touches my hair in my sleep

who will get the blood-stained yam
it's for us to decide
i shall write you a poem
then ask moses for a path
along which we can look
for each other

HAUNANI KAY TRASK

Haunani Kay Trask is Professor of Hawaiian Studies at the University of Hawai'i, and served for ten years as the Director of the University of Hawai'i's Center for Hawaiian Studies. She is also one of the founders and leading members of Kalahui Hawai'i, the largest native sovereignty organisation in Hawai'i. She has represented Hawai'i's indigenous people at the United Nations Working Group on Indigenous Peoples in Geneva, and at numerous indigenous gatherings in Samiland (Norway), Aotearoa (New Zealand) and Indian nations throughout the United States and Canada. She has published many articles on the struggle for self-determination of Hawai'i's indigenous people, and books, including *From a Native Daughter: Colonialism and Sovereignty in Hawai'i*. She served as a scriptwriter and co-producer of the award-winning documentary film *Act of War: The Overthrow of the Hawai'ian Nation*.

The Broken Gourd

I

After the last echo
where fingers of light
soft as laua'e
come slowly

toward our aching earth,
a cracked ipu
whispers, bloody water
on its broken lip.

Long ago, wise kānaka
hauled hand-twined
nets, whole villages shouting
the black flash of fish

Wāhine u'i
trained to the chant
of roiling surf;
nā keiki sprouted by the sun
of a blazing sky.

Even Hina, tinted
by love, shone gold
across a lover's sea.

II

This night I crawl
into the mossy arms
of upland winds,

an island's moan
welling grief:

Each of us slain
by the white claw
of history: lost
genealogies, propertied
missionaries, diseased
haole.

Now, a poisoned pae'āina
swarming with foreigners

and dying Hawaiians.

III

A common horizon:
smelly shores
under spidery moons,

pockmarked maile vines,
rotting ulu groves,
the brittle clack
of broken lava stones.

Out of the east
a damp stench of money
burning at the edges.

Out of the west
the din of divine

violence, triumphal
destruction.

At home, the bladed
reverberations of empire.

Kona Kaiʻōpua

Across a fathomless horizon,
koa voyaging canoes

plumed Kanaloa,
provocative summer clouds

gilded by the god:
blue pearl, green
olivine. In the Kona

noon, a lone naiʻa –
sea-sleek kinolau
of divinity.

Between coastal heiau
castrated niu, shorn

of fruit and flower,
fawning. From the ancestral
shore, tlack-tlack

of lava stones, massaged
by tidal seas: eternal
kanikau for long

forgotten aliʻi, entombed
beneath grandiose hotels
mocked

by crass amusements
Japanese machines
and the common greed

of vulgar Americans.

Pūowaina: Flag Day

for Ka'iana, Lākea, Mililani, Hulali, and Kalai'ola'a

Bring ginger, yellow
and white, broken stalks
with glossy leaves.

> Bring leihulu,
> palapalai, pikake. Bring
> kapa, beaten fine

> > as skin. Bring
> > the children
> > to chant

> > > for our dead,
> > > then stand
> > > with the lāhui

> > > > and burn
> > > > their American
> > > > flag.

Gods of my Ancestors

I sing of time before,
> ka wā mamua

> true, love-struck
> > engraved in song,
> > > in moon-woven palms
> > along luminous falls.

> I sing of the far green sea
> > ka moauli
> > > undulating
> > > > our great gods ascending.

I sing of mana
> the many-flanked Ko'olau
in the darkest blue dawn;
> the fierce foliage
> > of Kāne abundant:

'ohe, ulu, kalo
'ama'u

I sing of Pele
she who fires islands:
hāpu'u, lehua, 'ōlapa

I sing of Akua
Papa-hānau-moku
dense lava mother
swept by storm.

I sing of Hawai'i
'āina aloha

my high dark land
in flames.

Night is a Sharkskin Drum

Night is a sharkskin drum
sounding our bodies black
and gold.

All is aflame
the uplands a shush
of wind.

From Halema'uma'u
our fiery Akua comes:

E, Pele e,

E, Pele e,

E, Pele e,

From Ka'a'awa to Rarotonga

rainswept banana groves
    under a burdened sky

    refreshed by smells
        of seawind, blowing

        clouds to breadfruit islands,
            my tribal spirit

            dreaming flight,
                from Ka'a'awa
                    to Rarotonga

                    high-soaring 'iwa
                        plying the Pacific
                          with Maui's hook

Into our light I will go forever

Into our light
    I will go forever.

    Into our seaweed
        clouds and saltwarm
            seabirds.

Into our windswept
    'ehu kai, burnt
        sands gleaming.

        Into our sanctuaries
            of hushed bamboo,
                awash in amber.

Into the passion
    of our parted Ko'olau
        luminous vulva.

    Into Kāne's pendulous
        breadfruit, resinous
            with semen.

Into our wetlands
    of He'eia,
        bubbling black mud.

Into our spangled,
blue-leafed taro,
flooded with wai.

Into Waiahole,
chattering with rains
and silvered fish.

Into our shallows
of Kualoa,
translucent Akua.

Into the hum of
reef-ringed Ka‘a‘a‘wa,
pungent with limu.

Into our corals of
far Kahana, sea-cave
of Hina.

Into our chambered
springs of Punalu‘u,
ginger misting.

Into the songs of
lost La‘ie, cool
light haunting.

Into murmuring
Malaekahana,
plumed sands chanting.

Into the sheen
of flickering Hale‘iwa,
pearled with salt.

Into the wa‘a of
Kanaloa, voyaging
moana nui.

Into our sovereign suns,
drunk on the mana
of Hawai‘i.

KALONI TU'IPULOTU

Kaloni Piliniuote Tu'ipulotu was born in 1975 in Tonga, where she was educated and works as an economics teacher at Tonga High School. She received a university scholarship to go to New Zealand where she studied business and economics in Gisborne. She is a member of the Mataliki Tongan Writer's Group and writes poems in English and Tongan.

The Evil Woman

She is   H . . . . . u . . . . . g . . . . . e
Fat and white
With some nifo ali
A black "holy" smile
Married once but
Single now

Black clothes
Are her uniform
To school
To town
To church

Yes! She is a churchgoer
Who is known
To be the one
With the world's
Widest smile

Who always makes sure
That every individual
MISTAKE
Is broadcast
As headlines

On the radio
On the TV
And everywhere

"Typical of Coconut Wireless"
Some people say

One Sunday I was forced
To go to church
To avoid total interruption
I sat right in
The front seat

Suddenly I came to fix
My eyes on her!
Not for long
She looked away
With that mocking frowning face

"Something wrong?" I asked
To my conscience
Then there she went

She flung up
Off her seat
And shouted at me

"Go to the back,
That's the Minister's
Daughter's seat!"
I slowly moved away
With wonders,
Why, why? Oh! Why?
Is it a crime to be mis-seated?
Or is it a Sin
To sit in front
Without being labelled
And without that qualification?

HONE TUWHARE

Born in Kaikohe, New Zealand in 1922, Hone Tuwhare is of Ngā Puhi descent. His first poetry collection, *No Ordinary Sun*, was published in 1964 and he has since published *Selected Poems* (1980), *Year of the Dog: Poems New and Selected* (1982), *Mihi: Collected Poems* (1987), *Short Back and Sideways: Poems & Prose* (1992), *Deep River Talk* (1993), and *Shape-Shifter* (1997). He was awarded the Burns Fellowship in 1974 and his play, "In the Wilderness Without a Hat", was published in *He Reo Hou: 5 Plays by Maori Playwrights* (1991). In 1999 Hone Tuwhare was named New Zealand's second Te Mata Poet Laureate and in 2001 published *Piggy-back Moon*, which won the poetry category in the 2002 Montana New Zealand Book Awards.

With all things and with all beings we are as relative

Sunlight through the window falls
    on a pot-plant just breaking out
    in flower on the table.

    For a moment the flower
    is itself, complete.
    Which, of course, is a fiction.
    The flower gets its nourishment
    from the sun, and from me.

I will sing to it – chat it up.
    I will give it porridge-water to drink
    thin and cloudy. And today I might even
    celebrate its birth with an aria
    flamboyant and breathy.

    If I am as constant as the sun
    the moon and tide, the flower will die
    and I shall will it to bud again.

    Ten thousand times live to die; die
    and live again. And this is normal, quite
    acceptable; timely.

But who accepts as easily
    his own brief life as ebb and flow?
    As part of waxing and waning?
    As part of coming and going away
    Of sun and flower, moon and tide?

Grand-daughter Polly Peaches

There's no time between
now and my transition
to say goodbye to you.

Goodbye? Waste of time.

There's not enough room left
on the upturned butter-box
for your impetuous body
to come crashing alongside.

Oh, you'll damn me forever
for being kingly and remote –
for not granting you
a special audience: No

you may NOT sit on my knees.
You don't KNOW how swiftly
they grow numb when blood
flow is cut off.

It's good out here in the sun.

But, there IS a special need for me
to concentrate on each cell
and tube of me; listen to them
burble, and squeak, and sigh: All
systems go; or, just going,
thanks. And soon, soon

I shall be as deaf as stone
to all but the Hallelujah voices
of starched and whitened angels
swingin', "Abide with me" with
a tasty back-up by ol' Satchmo Louis
Armstrong, white handkerchief, mute
and horn – and when those Saints come
stompin' in, well, I ask you –

Now, be a good child and piss off, will ya?

Pith off, y'thelf, Gwun-dud.

Sun o (2)

Gissa smile Sun, giss yr best
good mawnin' one, fresh 'n cool like

yore still comin' – still
half in an' half outa the lan'scape?

An' wen yore clear of that eastern rim
of hills an' tha whole length of tha

valley begins to flood wit yr light, well
that's wen I could just reach out 'n stroke

tha pitted pock-marked pores of yr shiny
skin an' peel ya – just like a orange, right

down to yr white under-skin, but I wouldn't
bite ya – well, not until the lunch-bell goes

at noon wen I can feel ya hot an' outa reach
an' balanced right there – above my head.

C'mon, gissa smile Sun.

Yes

I like the Way
you slip out
of your things
pausing
between zip and
catch of breath
as if you were
punctuating
a movement: a phrase
of love. God

it cheers me
when you move with
purpose: animal
grace and awareness
of the urgency with
which agents
of locomotion take

us from a to z
table to bed and
back to the floor
again: hip hip

Yes: and I love
the way our limbs
construct
a superstructure
to a heavenly
accommodation: cheers

me no end

Salvaged

I too, am not inured to pain –
    the pangs of jealousy – the huff
    the puff, of cry-wounds.

We refashion newly, the misshapen
    allegories of love – with one
    red rose – furtive,
    among the groceries.

    And may I divulge that I, craftily
    have hid that special tankard
    rich, brimful

    of memories – from which no other
    lips but ours, have sipped: no
    other love, eclipsed.

Wry song

O may the texture
and fissured lines in
stone temper my life-style
to another self, enduring:
less faceless.

For in the tumult of my
separate hells, pummelled
I have been beyond shine or
recognition.

And if I should never know
delight again, or shut my
ears to coarse banalities
of sea and storm

then let my poems rock
to a dark sea's roll: as the
stricken moon.

God's Day to you too, Tree

The tree is not the same tree
    as it was yesterday.
    The tree is preening itself:
    it has grown two millimetres.
    It is showing off a brand new
    family of leaves this morning.
The tree wants to put on a good face
    for the Sun's advent. Her leaves
    bristle and tingle with high
    expectations.
The tree wants its hair combed
    differently today – east to west.
The tree is mildly irritated: the wind has
    creeped up behind, drawing cruel
    icy fingers up and down its cold
    southern flank.
Godday! says the Wind, familiarly. You wanna
    blow job, then?
    And God's Day to you, too. I want a
    blow wave, says the tree distantly
    muttering, rough bastard.

A Hongi for you too, Spring

no matter how many times you fall
in love – it is always for the first
time and – regularly, like perennially?

well, i've just been felled
(on my hands and knees) by your green
beauty, your fur – wet and shiny –
your scents

hey! somebody – please introduce
me to this first tiny multi-coloured
blaze in my bare patch of earth
kindling and tingling and doing
a switch on me up out of the frosty soil
and from low-profile leaves to bloomin'
flowers: magic all right.

Well
I get up off my wettened knees wiping
my dew-wettened nose to speak to the small
patch of colour more sanely in a Mihi
of Greeting . . .
i walk up and down in front of it – eyes
pinned to it (eyes righting, eyes lefting
like the way they drilled us in the army
to salute bowlegged colonels. Well, i prefer
the real kernels – multicoloured gifts from
our Earth Mum – sustenance for body, heart
and the soul) i'll make a start now, by
clearing goobie from my throat, first —
humming and haa-ing like a second-rate
orator of the old school —
(just thieving more time to compose)
I begin –
Um . . . . . there's been no official
word that i know of – to announce
your itsy-bitsy coming, SPRING . . . . so
do you mind if I just leap up and do
a haka to proclaim it – send a poem

to my friends? W O O O O - H O O O O !
Whiti . . . whiti . . . whīti! Whītiki-tia TE RAAA!

Fifteen Minutes in the Life of Johannes H. Jean Ivanovich

It's noon, already. My back and shoulders are bare, and i can feel
     the Sun nibbling me there – concentrated and thorough.

I'm pegging my clothes up on the line and thinking about what left-
     overs I could give away to my neighbour's dog, or heat up for
     my own lunch. My clothes don't look as if they'd been washed.
     It's time I changed my brand of washing-powder. Coyly, I turn
     the holey side of my underpants away from my neighbour's window
     doubling and pegging it up with a smooth, I-don't-give-a-shit-flourish.

I turn around to face the Sun puffing my chest out, my belly in. My
     shorts drop down past my pito exposing some fringe-hair growing on
     my very own Mount of Eden where the original Battle of the Bulge
     really took place.

I toss the leftover pegs in the empty basin, walking back with it to
     the Crib at the front of the section. I own one sixth of an acre.
     I can't get used to it. Earth Mum can't be owned by selfish indi-
     viduals. Secretly, I feel like a land-owning middle-class Kulak.

If I owned One Sixth of the World, I should be a high-up rangatira
     capitalist (living in the Kremlin) with lotsa classy woolly under-
     wear flying triumphantly on the flagstaff in Moskva, and spelling
     out the message: UP THE INTERNATIONAL WORKING CLASS! The Navy
     flagstaff at Waitangi has set a great historical precedence – for
     the whole World – in enhancing the technique – brilliantly – of
     underpants-waving.

Right now, the only Land Rights I can claim for sure – are lodged be-
     tween my toes. I recognise my real mates, Maori AND Pakeha.
     Heaps of them. They own NO real property to speak of. You'll
     find me – in them. It's Classy, neo-Classical. My true identity.

The Sun seems friendlier now, licking my chest, my belly. I can still
     feel the skin of my shoulder and back tightening – wincing creep-
     ily without any control I might have to stop it. I wonder if the
     Sun has remembered to extract its teeth from my back.

I go inside clicking the hot-water jug on, dumping the basin in the
     tiny separate shower/wash/toilet space, which I call: a Complex.
     I hitch up my shorts, wrapping a belt around me. The elastic
     around the waist-band of my shorts has perished. I think I shall
     live, though. A positive feeling I get in my water.

Laconically Canonical

It worries me now to buggerise around with
words designed to shape a panegyric to
our love, only to see it clomp up the creek
in gumboots ungainly – losing itself in
a messy puddle of the sticky stuffs binding
us together in an unholy composition that is
musically inept, lacking intensity and grunt

Your body is an
unconscious element of movement
and poise that could only be a feminine
endowment – a gift empowered with an
eloquence that is a river which may yet

Burst its banks of sensual arrogance
merging friendly in an incoherent sea
of mutual love squeals, squalls, moans
sigh . . . oh

Blessed are we simply for being ourselves
differently equipt, and for the sudden
intensity, interest, pleasure, ardour – the
mutual discovery and delight with the hearts'
whump working as one – and going bloody
well for us just now, I reckon

Bingo

Listlessness isn't a reflection of the heart's inaction
    On the contrary, when grief inhabits the desolate
    house, the heart is at its most irrepressible.
    It mirrors with empathy – the face, clenched
    unmindful of tears coursing down – side-tracked
    by the horizontal flesh-runnels, the bumps
    and knobs of the face, screwed up and bunched
    in anguish. The heart's scowl, yip and puppy-yowl
    help only to deepen the silence of the room
    wherein lies the Beloved, diffident, indifferent
    a moulded imperfection of sculptured stillness.
    And yet –

Out of the ancient fog of memory
  and in response to a salvaged dirge chanted
  by the white-haired Elder, the curtained eyes
  of the Beloved flicker – open briefly, briefly
  imploring silently, but expressively – before closing again.

The white-haired Elder has observed this
  rare phenomenon – with one other
  standing and leaning against the wall.

Without further ado, the grey-haired Elder, querulous, declares –
  'I have just received a sign, that in the long journey
  down to the waiting arms of the Mother that is Earth
  our dearly Beloved must be accompanied. Who among
  you is the Beloved's closest relative? But I leave this
  matter – to sort out among yourselves.'

A shudder
  like a small earth-tremor passes through the relatives
  of the Beloved, as each one privately reviews their kinship ties:
  a distant relative (and Clown) screams –

'*Bingo!*
  – Must be ME, ay?'
  Every one smiles. The problem is solved . . .
  Or . . . has it been . . .

The kitchen bell summons us to table.
  Two guardians are left behind to play guitar, croon
  to the Beloved. In the meantime
  in hearty reverence, we pay deference to
  our empty bellies.

View from a Furtive Hide

Just outside the eastern side of your dining-room
  window, the wind has abandoned a demeanour
  of insularity by remarking a presence, boisterously
  intermittent – cuffing the slender,
  green-eared bushiness of young saplings –
  testing, stretching their elasticity to indeterminate
  limits – their flowers remind me of penguins, yellow-
  eyed; bobbing, cavorting – a comical two-step with a

black unchoreographed beat of floppy-tailed
Chaplinesque dawdles. All to the wild wind's whip. O,

let the sun's rays unwind me. Wind me unkink –
straighten out; warm . . .

My Pork & Puha Anthem

My mirror angled low, swivels on two upright
    props fixed firmly to the back of my dresser –
    At this angle of tilt, the mirror is reflectively
    focused instead on my hairiness – just below
    my pito – and notable only for the evidence of
    tell-tale streaks of greyness in among my bush – or,
    the blush of graininess there (to put a
        kindlier twist to my masculinity). Well, who the
        hell else is going to give a damn? I love me;
        my cheeky 'Oldie'-ness.
        Well, I'm not into tilting the crap out of windmills.

I tilt the mirror. My face leaps out more squarely
    into view. I'm not enthused. It's my face, alright,
    but it's not infused with that inner spread of
    joy and satisfaction it wears after a feast of
    pork-bones, puha – and, *O, boy* – dough boy!

Ahhh . . . what religious gifts of beautification Nature
    gives to us, in all her colourful variety, of wheaten
    and green produce – the wild ones unsown by
    human hands, together with the domesticated
    porker sans grunt; and its high-pitched scream
    before getting its throat cut. I betake myself –
    by getting off my arse to arrange a musical
    scherzo of kitchenware / a saucepan filled with
    herbal / meatie nourishment, coming to the boil. O yea!

EMMA KRUSE VAAI

Emma Kruse Vaai was born and raised in Samoa. As well as a poet, she is also a writer of short stories. She and her husband Alo Vaimoa Vaai have four children.

Mango Mission

Branches laden
with sweet succulent mangoes
so heavy with juice
so tempting
on a hot useless afternoon

Old man Vili is drinking his tea
he won't see
with his back turned shall we? shall we?
Sinners, stealers of mangoes shall be burned in hell
but for now let it be

You take the stick
I'll hold out my t-shirt
don't make a noise
just aim at the stems

one, two, three . . .
uou! uou! uou!
oh shiti the dog the dog
your squealer shit dog
uou! uou! WHO'S THAT?
SON OF A BITCH – GITOUTA THERE!
bellows Vili with his back turned.
Quick! run! he has a gun!
Kick that shit squealer spoiler dog
run! run! before Vili gets his gun!

Such sweet succulent mangoes
unfortunately only two
one for you and one for me
on a hot sinful afternoon

Prescription

Gather some sunshine
and warm rain
one cicada
and a pocket of air from your kitchen
a pot pourri of frangipani, sandalwood, mosooi
and gardenia
into a parcel
with a long letter
airmail
to me
from you
home in Samoa

Returning

(Jacky Kolhase Lenz)

so there you are back
on the island
speaking German
to your kids
catching up
with old friends
and rellies
my how things have changed you say
and some old folks saying
some things never change on this island
and it's not just Jim Reeves and Elvis Presley
immortalised on Radio 2AP

so there you are back
on the island
talking about Haus and Garten
so did your sixth form Latin help you
weather that cold German language
Do you also say "Oh table" in German?
Mensa mensa mensam
amo amas amat
I wonder if such chants
will feature in our senility

so there you are back
on the island
only to visit
not to stay
to soak up some island sun
and warm rain
to let your children
see your other side
through your family,
through your friends
the trees, the hills,
the sea and the sky
and in the winter
far away from here
sit in front of your fireplace
and stay warm in the thought
of umu fires burning
and remember.

Tropical Fantasia

Cinderella mornings
wrapped in snow white mist
Rapunzel is washing
her lovely long hair
at the falls of Papase'ea
The mother is angry
and wielding a coconut broom
because her son Siaki has sold their cow
for a handful of beans at the Savalalo market
The skinny dog with hungry saucer eyes
yawns beside a tinder box called Siva Afi
while Sleeping Beauty poisoned
with guava apples
reposes on her fluffy kapok bed
under which there's a can of Watties green peas

Today I shall be the little mermaid on the beach
when all my chores are complete.

ALBERT WENDT

Albert Wendt CNZM is of the Aiga Sa-Tuaopepe of Lefaga, the Aiga Sa-
Maualaivao of Malie, and the Aiga Sa-Patu of Vaiala, Samoa. Poet, novelist,
short-story writer and playwright, he is currently a Professor of English
specialising in New Zealand and Pacific Literatures and Creative Writing at the
University of Auckland. He has been an influential figure in the developments
that have shaped New Zealand and Pacific literature since the 1970s. He is the
author of five novels, three books of short stories, three previous collections of
poetry, articles on Pacific writing and art, and the editor of two major
anthologies of Pacific writing.

The Mountains of Ta'ū

Mountains wouldn't be
mountains without the valleys   ravines
and sea level they rise up from
They are
the rising high of sight propped up by stone
earth and sky
They can't be
any other thing (and they know it)
They are
the eyes of the earth   gazing out
gazing inwards   contemplating the future
on the horizon line and in the depths
of the whirling retina

These mountains   the mountains of Ta'ū   are
locked arm to arm   blood to blood
and live in one another's thoughts

They hum
like spinning tops or Maui's endlessly
inventing mind   on fine mornings
when the mist lifts and the horizons open
to the promise of what may be

They creak and crack
like old aoa trees   as they dry in the sun
and the river dives and digs
for its roots   and
fat pigeons nibble the day away on
the sweet black berries of moso'oi   and
in cold rock pools Atua wash off
the night's stale smell of sex and perfume
their twisting hair with laumaile leaves and
for dear life trees and creeper cling onto
sharp slope and cliff and the air
is thick with long messages of death
in the falling

They whisper together in the evenings
in talk only they can hear
as the dark turns all languages
into one shape of the tongue   and
the ravenous flyingfox chases
the ripe-papaya moon   and
comic aitu squeal in the waterfall

They sleep best
on stormy nights when they can't hear
one another's sleep-chatter
and the wind massages their aching spines
with tender hands

These mountains   the mountains of Ta'ū   are
above the violence of arrogant men
They now fit my eyes and heart exactly
like a calm river is snug in the hand
of its bed
I am of their rising
I am of their dreaming
and they of mine

These mountains   the mountains of Ta'ū

Aunt's Gallery

The walls of my aunt's sitting room at Malie
were a crowded gallery of family photographs
As I grew the collection grew and changed arrangement
One photo never lost its central position though
It held the heart of the main wall
A small black and white portrait of her father
Gaunt face – prominent forehead – penetrating eyes
searching for what he would never find
Everyone said I looked like him
But even my aunt wouldn't divulge much about him
Years later I found out he'd died of alcohol
not long after that photo was taken
He was only thirty-six

Uncle Sanerivi – aunt Ita's first husband
was one of the first Samoans to be taken
by the LMS to London and trained for the ministry
I grew up with a row of his photographs in my aunt's house
My favourite is of him standing stiffly upright
in a black tie black suit black trousers
holding his black bowler hat against his chest
(The Noble Savage so correctly English!)
Faint impish smile aimed at the future
with Ita and four children
and fame throughout the country for
his sermons intellect and humility
He didn't live to see Vaiese and her husband
work as missionaries in New Guinea
or his youngest son – Aleni – become
a professional wrestler instead of the pastor
our Aiga sent him to New Zealand to become
or Ioane the eldest as Minister of Finance
I've always admired his immaculate handwriting
in the exercise books he filled with our Aiga's gafa
and left to Ita to protect for my generation

In my aunt's gallery there were three photos of me
One the enlarged passport head of a thirteen-year-old
smiling bravely but I remember was shitscared
of the journey to New Zealand and boarding school
Three years later I'm capped and in full school uniform
on the veranda of Niger House wearing the Wendt frown

as I look out of the frame at Mt Taranaki
(My mother had died the year before)
In the third photo I'm standing with cousin Pine
at a party in Auckland aswirl with cigarette smoke
our beer glasses raised to the camera
Whenever my children stayed with Ita
she used those photographs to teach them
an exemplary history of their father
and warn them of the evils of drinking
She was accurate in her predictions:
last week my cousin Pine died of cirrhosis of the liver
after a lifetime of enjoying the liquid demons
Since university I've had a career of bleeding ulcers
caused so my aunt has argued by those same demons

During the three days of her burial rituals
when hundreds of aiga and friends gathered
her family of photographs disappeared from the walls
When I was at university she promised me Sanerivi's
books of gafa but they too vanished during her funeral

Te One-Roa-a-Tohe

We tried but no camera can take in one shot
the whole stretch of Te One-Roa-a-Tohe as it paths
the spirits of the Dead up to Te Reinga
(Reina's Dead from Murihiku journey here too)
We saw the flax bending as the spirits passed
Heard them whispering among the dunes
and their rustling in the manuka

Later we stood in front of the lighthouse
and photographed the sacred pohutukawa
down on the precarious eastern face of the headland
I imagined the spirits leaping from it
into the prophetic current that will carry them
to Hawaiki where the ancestral explorer Kupe came
from to name and detail Maui's Ika
We photographed each other against the immense sky
Ahead the Tasman and the Pacific embraced
in turbulent whirlpools

In Samoa my Dead gather at the Fafa at Falealupo
where the La sets and the Po begins
On the beach   the men bath in one rock pool
the women in the other then they walk
the lava path into the sea and dive for Pulotu
Falealupo is the home of the Atua Nafanua
who ruled for three hundred years
until the first Catholic priests converted Her congregation
You can still visit the lava cave where
pilgrims through Her divining taulaaitu
sought Her help and prophecies
Once with Soifua   Her Tuua   I visited Her temple –
a tiered pyramid of stones and boulders
now overgrown with forest and Christianity
(No one dares clear Her refuge)
For that long sad silence that weaves all things
She held us in Her green gaze
In times of trouble the matai council still meets
at night in Soifua's maota
They leave one row of blinds facing the west raised
for Nafanua to enter for the inventive consultation
Her direct descendant is now Cardinal of Polynesia
Outlawed atua have surprising ways of conquering the present

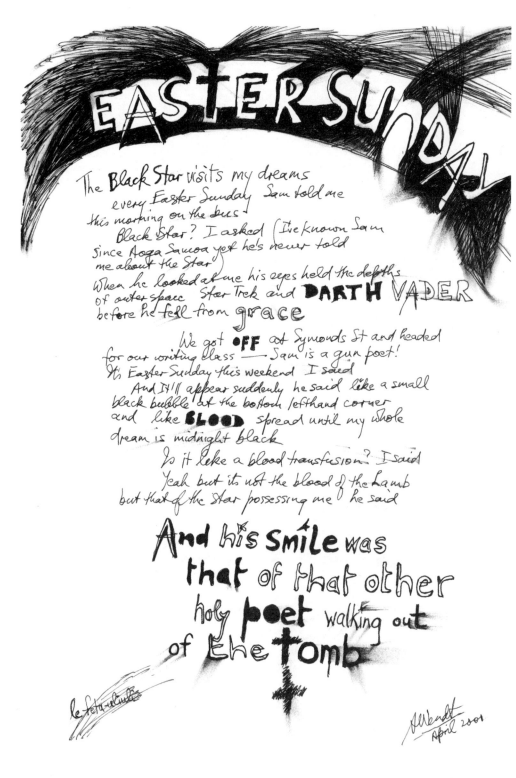

EASTER SUNDAY

The Black Star visits my dreams
    every Easter Sunday Sam told me
this morning on the bus
    Black Star? I asked (I've known Sam
since Aoga Samoa yet he's never told
me about the Star)
When he looked at me his eyes held the depths
of outer space   Star Trek and DARTH VADER
before he fell from grace

        We got OFF at Symonds St and headed
for our writing class —— Sam is a gun poet!
It's Easter Sunday this weekend I said
    And It'll appear suddenly he said like a small
black bubble at the bottom lefthand corner
and like BLOOD spread until my whole
dream is midnight black
        Is it like a blood transfusion? I said
        Yeah but its not the blood of the Lamb
but that of the Star possessing me he said

And his smile was
that of that other
holy poet walking out
of the tomb

le fetu-uli-mt

Albadt
April 2001

— 251 —

over
PONSONBY
over
PONSONBY

Last night just before
dawn while the cold fo-
raged thru' our backyard,
the **BLACK STAR**
hovered above PONSONBY
right over our house.
Yeah, it was like
CLOSE **ENCOUNTERS**
OF THE *THIRD KIND*
+ I opened my window to It,
Sam sd. Yeah
and opened my PORES
to ITs converting LIGHT
+ deep scent of SPACE-
travel, oceans without-end,
+ GOD.
But you don't believe in God,
I sd
NOW I do, he smiled

Alexander April 2001

SITE

This autumn morning our one-way
street is a stream of weaving light
that hurts my eyes as I try to site it
on this page
It escapes down to
JOHN ST + at
the junction divides
+ dances left + right
iNTO all the Ponsonby
streets
+ eyes that try to
SITE IT...
Such is the LIGHT's
QUEST for
Location

AWendt
May 2001

STRETCH

So you want to stretch to stretch out like a sail + catch ALL the people you LOVE?

A Wendt
July 2001

— 254 —

CREATURES

Every night just BEFORE DAWN
the dark faceless creatures seep
into his dreams
circle SQUAT + watch him
watching them
BLACK LIGHT cauled in the language
of BIRTH
they smell of ancient quests across
the VANIMONIMO
of ancestral veins that connect BONE
to FLESH to STAR to ATUA
Theirs is the long SAD SILENCE before
TAGALOAALAGI uttered
the FIRST WORD
+ gave TONGUE to our pain
HIS is the silence of wonder

As DAWN DANCES across
PONSONBY + WINTER
he wakes to his CREATURES
waving goodbye
WITHOUT HANDS

Albert
July 2001

SPIRAL out + out into our eyes to heal our wounds as they blur our tears they SPIRAL out as they doesn't IT DOESN'T LACK the BLACK have A HEART STAR forgets it the SOMEtimes forgets sometimes

RICHARD WILCOX

Prison Mouse

It was here in Eden Prison at the turn of eighty-six
On remand dreading judgment in this place where inmates mix
Feeling kind of lonely I was celled up all alone
So to help me with the boredom I then started writing poems
Now this one which is now written is a classic in itself
Put down on to paper just to tell you how I felt
When suddenly my eyes beheld one very eerie sight
Something small and evil slipped beneath my big steel door
Then slowly made its way across my cold, hard, concrete floor
I tried so hard to focus on the intruder in my house
When suddenly it dawned on me this creature was a mouse
And so from one's close inspection I had seen him kinda fat
Kind of broad across the shoulders and quicker than a cat
He then strode toward my safe box, to where my goods were stored
Chose himself a block of cheese then grabbed for something more
Hell I didn't mind that block of cheese 'cause I had two or three
It was when he snapped my happy weed he had made an enemy
So I eased up off my cold hard bunk as quietly as I could
Then jumped down off my metal bed and he froze right where he stood
Well I've gotta tell you matey I really thought I had his ass
But this furry little creature was super lightning class
He then jumped into a corner then reared up on the seat
and lifting up his tiny paws he had no signs of defeat
So I threw a right hand swiftly that threw him to the door
Busted two or many ribs and fractured his right jaw
I then kicked him in the stomach heard him groan then kicked again
We battled over happy weed hell! I thought it would never end
Then I was about to give more pressure that would bring him to demise
When suddenly I noticed tiny teardrops in his eyes
He then yells go on Mr inmate go ahead and take my life
'Cause being a prison mouse you see has been all hell and strife
Well to tell the truth I spun out when I heard this small mouse talk
'Cause I thought that I heard stranger things before I could even walk
Then this little furry creature runs a story down on me
He says before you waste me Mr here's something you should see
He folded up his prison sleeve and extended one front paw
And then I saw a tattooed patch with lettering and all

Well I was made down in the sewers and my father was a rat
He bashed me nearly every day but I shan't go into that
I got caught out stealing goodies from another inmate's cell
Now I wish this guy had killed me cause my life's a living hell
But instead he had me pinching smoke while inmates were away
And now that's the kind of work I do right to this very day
Well, so one night he started drinking homemade brew you see
And for the lack of nothing else to do this pea brain spotted me
He yanked me from my cardboard box and dumped me on the floor
Busted six or many ribs and fractured my left paw
Well finally he crashed out so I cut a track from there
Then caught a jigger from Kaitoke and made my way up here
I tried to follow the straight and narrow but it got me put inside
And being a prison mouse you see guess I'm institutionalised
So close your powerful hands now buddy cause I ain't afraid to die
Then he looked at me with saddened eyes and then began to cry
Hell, I couldn't do it matey I kept thinking what he said
Gee my old man always bashed me up and rearranged my head
So I released his tiny body and watched him cross the floor
It only took him a second or two to slip beneath my door
He then walked out onto the landing to see if the way was clear
And I noticed that his tiny face was now quite free of fear
And instead upon his evil mug he wore the meanest grin
And these last few words he shot at me knew what a fool I'd been
Why you bloody stupid boobhead why for you a waste of fists
Your life is one big joke to me that even I can't miss
And last of all you dickhead take some advice that's true
Get your act together or they'll make a queer out of you
Then this furry creature flipped me off and strutted on his way
Disappearing out of view before I had my say
I know I should be spewing mate but in a way I'm not
For this bloody little creature had taught me quite a lot
So now my warning to you boobheads doing time behind these walls
Perhaps one day you'll catch this mouse with the tattoo on his paw
And when you do remember me and show him some respect
Tell him that you've read my poem, then break his scrawny neck!

BRIAR WOOD

Briar Wood grew up in Mangere in Auckland, and is currently Senior Lecturer in Creative Writing, New Literatures, Cultural and Critical Theory at London Metropolitan University. She is a graduate of the University of Auckland and has a DPhil from the University of Sussex. She has worked as a journalist and editor. Her poetry and critical writing has been widely published. In 2001 she wrote poems for the "Glorified Scales" installation by Maureen Lander at Te Papa Whakahiku/The Auckland War Memorial Museum, which referred to their Ngā Puhi whakapapa.

Saccharine Daddy

While mom earbashed me

on the drive home from Ronnie Scott's
slumped drunk in a black cab
I remember you swayed to Nina Simone

humming *Put a Little Sugar in my Bowl*
Jamming the baby grand –
you were a stake
against which I leaned,
unruly scarlet runner bean.

What a squat solid citizen.
Portly barrel you rattled on
in that soiled suede overcoat
and Joseph Stalin rasp.

Hate was too puling a word –
I tried to despise your blind adoration
for anything and everything American.
Barracuda through and through.

Chainsaw massacres took place
in the back seat of the family sedan
as you abused your fellow drivers,
face beaming like neon.

Agamemnon's death mask.
Pills and a diet
for high blood pressure
No more pavlova.

All Papa Meilland heart,
red cabbage patches
and pandering to grandsons.

Then again just for the record

a Nat King Cole version of
Moonlight in Vermont
on Sunday evenings
as we kids riffed to sleep

For All We Know

Pomegranates

With a craving this persistent
I could be pregnant
but only want to conceive
a child. Waking to a breaking
wave of curved sunlight
waterlogged as flotsam.

These are the underground months.
It is just enough to ask
how to lose sight of dry land
in a history of daylight robbery.
When a cry for help might rebound
across the clearing clotted by violets
and what solitary witnesses tell
a mother who arrives too late
with ransacking of conscience.

The marketplace rages.
Sound is a mouthful of teeth.
Biting a hand grenade.
Swallowing more than can be chewed.
Jewelled cruelties. Spilling their guts.
Ineluctable. The word for more
rolling snugly on the tongue.
Blood from a stone.

Fork out for a pound or two
of hell fruit. Smouldering coals.
Hugging a basket of answers.
Ruby fluid trickles in the fissure
where hearts have their compartments.
Frog spawn. Borne on the river ride.
Arteries beat. Clustered streets.

Between the Flags

Surfers say
beware of calm surfaces

where feeder currents run.
Labour weekend, come Monday

the kowhai rains.
Apple orchard parabolas

in a transmarine season.
Magnetic iron sands at Muriwai

like walking in an advent calendar
thinking of dracaenas

punkish at Perrinporth.
Twinkling starfish.

Flutter boards buck
in the tumble of Tangaroa.

No household rubbish here.
Hillsides swept stark.

Manuka rumps to the wind.
Puhe's perfume, sunflushed air.

Floating off the coast –

Motutara

U Turn

Legging it home
in a neck to neck
finish blocking
each other's struggle
for leftovers in the fridge.
Brothers wrestling
to a double hitch
The Stranglers pumping
I Can Drive
My Very Own Tank
from bedroom stereos.
Boastful posters,
Bryan Williams striding,
Grant Batty's sidestep everywhere.
I was the orange girl
at half time.
Woken by three
to watch the Springboks
hoping the All Blacks
would thrash them.
Sobbing when Chris Laidlaw
got carried off by zambucks
No more glorious
teamwork
with Earl Kirton.
I could tell
a head high tackle
from a forward pass.
Growing in spurts.
Stubbed toes.
Mowed lawns.
Hassled for therapy
with girlfriend trouble.
perilous platforms
runner board
pick up
hotted up drop off
pash
   in someone's mother's mini
    the median strip
     a first fuck
      after two and a half bottles
       of Cold Duck
        while the windows   steamed up

the words are
burning rubber
cars on judder bars
Aorere
Otara Market
sparkling taro
Navel Oranges
lavalava gardens
milk bottle money
railway workshop whistle time
Friesian paddocks
wintergreen
methylated spirits
too much ultraviolet
surfing the runner board
across the causeway
to Puketutu
a GIVE WAY sign
Marama's kainga
morning talks
relay race
handing a baton
over to Lili
pews of covered buttons
nautical flares
missionary robes
crucifixed
cowries
power dressed
Milk Bar Queens
along St George St
nautical flares
airplay
Radio Hauraki
Selusalima's songs
teuteu
hoki mai hoki mai
titoki
Hokey pokey
Hokey pokey
The Mad Butchers
Mutton flaps
Tip Top Corner

Glossary

aganu'u	Samoan for lifestyle of a group, culture.
ahi	the sandalwood tree (*Santalum yasi*), the fragrant wood of which is used to scent coconut oil and for specialised wood carving (yasi in Fijian).
āholehole	the Hawaiian name of a particular silver-coloured reef fish.
aiga	Samoan for family (nuclear or extended).
'āina	land or earth, in Hawaiian, family.
'āina aloha	a Hawaiian phrase for beloved land.
aitu	a Samoan word for spirits.
ali'i	a Hawaiian term for chief.
'ama'u	fern, in Hawaiian.
aoa	a Samoan name for the banyan tree.
aroha	a Maori word meaning unconditional love, compassion, caring and concern, the ability to accept another reality without condemning it or trying to change it.
atua	a Samoan word for gods.
'awa	Hawaiian term for the Kava, a shrub native to Pacific islands, the root being the source of a narcotic drink of the same name.
'awapui	the Hawaiian word for white ginger.
'āweoweo	the Hawaiian name of a particular red-coloured reef fish.
awhina	Maori for help, support.
bula boys	gang of young Fijian men.
C.P.S.	Child Protective Services (Hawai'i).
dracaena	cabbage tree.
E kui	in New Zealand Maori, a form of address to a kuia or woman old enough to be your, or whom you regard as a, grandmother. A bit like saying "Gran" rather than "Grandmother."
E sa oe moa	Samoan for "You are sacred moa".
E te mana'o i se ipu ti?	Samoan for "Would you like a cup of tea?".
E tu, e tu, e tu, Tanemahuta	"Stay standing tall, Tanemahuta!" Tanemahuta is the Maori god of the forests and is embodied by all trees, birds and creatures of the forest.
eh kare	colloquial Maori for "hey mate".
'ehu	Hawaiian term for reddish tinged hair.
'ehu kai	a Hawaiian term for sea spray, foam.
fa'afafine	Fa'afafine is usually defined as "the way of a woman". It is cognate with the classic Tongan word "fakafafine" and related to the eastern Polynesian word "mahu". It refers to the practice of biological men living as "women" in Samoan culture. By "woman" one means actually a "femme" or "feminine". Fa'afafine do not identify as women or as gay men but as their own people, the Fa'afafine.
fa'alavelave	a wedding, a funeral, a birthday, any Samoan ceremony that requires people to come together and more importantly, to give for the common good; also refers to the food, money or gifts given at important family functions.
falahola	a sacred variety of pandanus (*Pandanus tectorius var sinensis*) the unusual male flowers or hingano of which are used in leis or to scent coconut oil. (Tonga).
fale	house, in Samoan.
fananga	Tongan term for legend.
fanku	a play on the words "thank you".
fetau	a tree commonly found on Pacific beaches.
gafa	a Samoan word for genealogy.
H.V.B.	Hawai'i Visitors Bureau.
hā	Maori term for the life breath.

haka	New Zealand Maori for an energetic dance.
hala	the Hawaiian name for pandanus (*Pandanus odoratissimus*).
hangi	New Zealand Maori term for an earth oven.
haole	Hawaiian for a white person, American, Englishman, Caucasian; formerly any foreigner.
haole hula	post-colonial hula, highly influenced by the commercial tourism industry, written in both English and Hawaiian, but reflecting American culture and values, as distinguished from traditional sacred hula.
hāpu'u	an endemic tree fern of the Hawaiian archipelago, found in abundance in forests at Kīlauea volcano.
harakeke	Maori for flax.
harirū	Maori for shake hands.
hau	a lowland Hawaiian tree; its bast is used for rope and canoe lashings.
haurangi	New Zealand Maori for drunk.
he'e	squid, in Hawaiian.
hehea	a small tree (*Syzygium corynocarpum*) the fragrant red or yellow fruit of which are used in garlands (misimisi in Fijian).
heiau	a temple of worship. Many temples existed in traditional Hawai'i, including large, elaborate temples for human sacrifice.
heilala	(*Garcinia sessilis*) the national flower of Tonga and considered sacred; used to make special garlands and to scent coconut oil.
himene tuki	Cook Island Maori for a polyphonic song style incorporating "grunting" sounds, based on biblical texts.
hingano	Tongan for the unusual male flowers of falahola, a sacred variety of pandanus (*Pandanus tectorius var sinensis*), which are used in leis or to scent coconut oil.
hoki mai	Maori for return.
hongi	in New Zealand Maori, to share the breath of life by pressing noses, or, by pressing you nose to something other than another human being which you wish to acknowledge in the same fashion.
hori	pejorative term for Maori; George.
hui	a New Zealand Maori word for a meeting or the people.
huni	a small coastal tree (*Phaleria disperma*), the flowers and leaves of which are used in garlands and to scent Tongan oil.
ika	fish.
ipu	a Hawaiian word for a gourd, or a drum made from a gourd.
ipu heke	a gourd drum with a top section.
'iwa	the Hawaiian name for the frigate bird.
iwi	a New Zealand Maori word for people, tribe; a Hawaiian word for bone. The bones of the dead, considered the most cherished possession, were hidden. The iwi contains the mana of an individual even in death.
J.K.B.	James K. Baxter, New Zealand poet.
ka kite	in Cook Island Maori, goodbye.
kā lā'au	in Hawaiian, a phrase for stick dancing; also refers to fencing.
ka moauli	a Hawaiian term for the dark blue sea.
ka raungaiti au	a New Zealand Maori phrase meaning "I am homesick and alone" (an illusion from the well known lyric "E Pa to Hau", as discussed by Trixie Menzies in "Appreciation of a Poem", *Landfall* 167).
ka wā mamua	a Hawaiian phrase meaning the time before: a reference to ancient times
kaha	New Zealand Maori for strength.
kai	food ("tucker" writes Keri Hulme), in New Zealand Maori.
kai karanga	the leading woman caller, as in Maori ceremonial encounters.
kainga	Maori for village.
kaitangata	New Zealand Maori for human flesh.
kai tiaki	guardian, in New Zealand Maori.
kakala	Tongan for garland, or a collection of fragrant parts of a plan especially flowers.

kalo	taro, a starchy tuber that is the staple of the Hawaiian diet; metaphorically, taro is the parent of the Hawaiian people.
kaloni kakala	Tongan for perfumed blossoms.
kānaka	the Hawaiian people.
kanikau	a Hawaiian term meaning dirge, lamentation, chant of mourning.
kapa	a Hawaiian word for cloth made from pounded bark, usually from wauke or mamaki bark, and imprinted with intricate designs; clothes.
kapa haka	traditional Maori songs/dances.
kape	a root crop, a member of the taro family. (Cook Islands)
kapu	a Cook Island Maori term for sacredness.
kapu moe	in Hawaiian, a prostration taboo, accorded highest ranking chiefs.
karakia	a word used in both New Zealand Maori and Cook Island Maori for prayer, poem or incantation.
karanga	in New Zealand Maori, a call that usually takes place as part of the powhiri (welcome), between a kuia or woman from the home people of the marae and a kuia or woman from the visiting party. The calls alternate back and forth, beginning with the home people, in order to acknowledge who everyone is, their dead, the links between them, the purpose of their meeting and anything else that is deemed appropriate by those doing the calling.
kare	a Cook Island Maori word meaning no.
kaumatua	a New Zealand Maori male elder, or elders versed in the traditions, histories and practices of the ancestors.
kauri	a New Zealand native tree, regarded by Maori as one of the greats of the forest.
kava	pounded root, served as ceremonial drink.
kawanatanga	a New Zealand Maori word for partial sovereignty. The word comes from the root transliteration for Governor, Kawana, so refers to the limited authority that is afforded a Governor.
kei te noa, ahua	a phrase in New Zealand Maori meaning I don't exist.
kia ora	an informal New Zealand Maori greeting.
kikau	in Cook Island Maori, the leaf of a coconut tree.
kina	New Zealand Maori word for sea-urchin, sea-egg.
kino lau	a Hawaiian term for the many forms taken by a god, such as the ti leaf as a form of the mo'o (lizard) god.
koa	a large, native Hawaiian forest tree with crescent-shaped leaves, which produces a fine red hardwood formerly used for canoes, now for furniture, calabashes and 'ukulele.
koha	Maori for donation, gift.
koho	Nuiean for fort, tower, look-out point.
koko laisa	transliteration from cocoa rice, a rice pudding made with coca.
kokowhai	red ochre. (Maori).
korero	Maori word for speech, conversation; also a Cook Island Maori word for culture or tradition.
koromiko	native New Zealand tree.
kowhai	yellow; native New Zealand tree.
kowhaiwhai	a New Zealand Maori word to describe the scroll work on rafters in meeting houses.
kuia	senior Maori woman.
kukui hele pö	a Hawaiian phrase for a lantern which burns the oil of the candlenut tree.
kulak	in the Soviet Union, a peasant working for their own profit.
kulukona	a now rare woody vine (*Alyxia bracteolosa*); has fragrant leaves and stems, used in leis and garlands like the Hawaiian maile.
kumara	sweet potato. (Maori).
kūmū	the Hawaiian word for the goatfish, a red reef fish.
kūpe'e	in Hawaiian, a bracelet or anklet made of animal teeth, i.e. boar, whale, or dog.
kupuna	the Hawaiian word for grandparent or ancestor.
kuriri	the Cook Island Maori word for a shore bird, the wandering tattler (*Heteroscelsus incanus*).

kūtai	Maori word for mussels
lāhui	a Hawaiian term meaning people, nation.
lākī	Ti leaf, in Hawaiian. Traditionally, this was used for protection.
langakali	one of Tonga's most sacred small trees (*Aglaia saltatorum*), the piercingly but fleetingly fragrant flowers of which are used in garlands and for scenting Tongan oil.
laua'e	a Hawaiian word meaning fragrant, native fern.
laumaile	a Samoan vine.
lavalava	Samoan wraparound garment.
le faa Samoa	the Samoan way.
lehua	the bright red, fuzzy flower of the ohi'a tree; symbol of Hawai'i island.
lei hulu	a Hawaiian term for a feather lei; formerly worn by royalty; a beloved child or person.
limu	in Hawaiian the general name for all plants living under water, salt or fresh.
LMS	London Missionary Society.
lo'i	Hawaiian for irrigated terrace, especially for taro.
lotu tamaiti	in Samoan this literally means children's church but in popular usage it refers to "White Sunday", one Sunday in October every year specially devoted to children.
maika'i	in Hawaiian, good; a good thing.
maile	a Hawaiian native twining shrub with fragrant, shiny leaves used for decoration and lei, especially reserved for the highest ceremonial occasions or honours.
makatea	in Cook Island Maori, the raised formation of dead coral around the coast of an island.
make	the Hawaiian word for death, to die.
mana	pan-Polynesian word meaning a miracle, presence, spirit, divine power, authority, prestige, inner strength.
Mana Maori Motuhake	New Zealand Maori independence, sovereignty or separate development, a Maori way of life that is different to and distinct from Pakeha or New Zealand European ways.
mana wahine	in New Zealand Maori, the strength, dignity and prestige of women, and their ability to respond appropriately to any situation.
mana'o	Hawaiian and Samoan term for desire.
maneaba	a village meeting house in Kiribati.
mango	a tropical fruit.
manuhiri	in New Zealand Maori, visitor or bird of passage.
manuka	New Zealand tea-tree.
maoli	indigenous people (Hawaiian)
maota	a Samoan term for the meeting house of a chief.
mapa	the fragrant (fleshy) fruit of the mapa tree used in a special garland. (Tonga)
marae	a New Zealand Maori word which comes from Te Marae-atea a Tumatauenga, meaning the space immediately before the whare nui or meeting house, and now used to refer to the entire complex, usually consisting of a whare nui (meeting house), whare kai (dining hall) and whare paku (ablutions block).
marangai	south or southeast wind. (Cook Islands).
matai	a Samoan word for chiefs; a New Zealand Maori word for a particular type of native tree.
mata'oi	the Cook Island Maori name for the ylang ylang tree (*Cananga odorata*). Its yellow spider-like flowers are used to scent coconut oil.
Mauli	inner being (Samoa).
maunga	Maori for mountain.
me aro koe ki te ha o Hineahuone	a New Zealand Maori whakatauki or proverb, meaning "pay heed to the strength that is women".
mea ai	Samoan for food.
mei	Tongan for breadfruit.
mene'une	in Cook Island Maori, tiny magical people, fairies (appropriated from the Hawaiian word menehune).
mere	hand-held weapon (Maori).
mihi	Maori word for greeting.

moa	Samoan for chicken, centre.
moana nui	a Hawaiian term meaning the deep ocean; literally, big sea.
mohokoi	Tongan tree bearing fruit the size and shape of olives.
moko	Maori tattoo.
mokopuna	New Zealand Maori for grandchildren.
mo'o	Samoan for gecko.
mo'okū'auhau	in Hawaiian, genealogy.
Moriori	indigenous people of the Chatham Islands
moso'oi	a Samoan tree that produces fragrant yellow flowers used for lei and for scenting coconut oil.
motutapu	New Zealand Maori for sacred island.
muka	inner fibrous part of flax; processed flax fibre (New Zealand Maori).
nā keiki	a Hawaiian word for children.
nā 'ōiwi	plural form of native, or native son; refers to the indigenous people of Hawai'i.
na'au	in Hawaiian, this literally means intestines or bowel; figuratively, it refers to the mind or heart, the place where one senses one's kupuna, or ancestors.
Nafanuā	Samoan warrior goddess.
nai'a	a Hawaiian word for porpoise.
naupaka	a Hawaiian native species of shrub found in the mountains and near coasts, famed for its white flowers that look like half-flowers; also a Hawaiian story of parted lovers.
ngahere	Maori word meaning native bush.
ngaio tree	native New Zealand tree
ngākau	Maori for heart, seat of affections.
nifo ali	Maori for lips.
ni'oi	the Cook Island Maori word for an evergreen shrub which bears edible red berries (*Eugenia reinwardtiana*).
niu	a Hawaiian word for the coconut palm; a male symbol.
N.W.A.	Niggers With Attitude, an American rap group.
'ohana	family, in Hawaiian.
'ohe	the Hawaiian word for bamboo.
'ōlapa	several native Hawaiian species of forest trees with green leaves that flutter like aspen leaves; a dancer as contrasted with the chanter; a dance accompanied by chanting and drumming on a gourd drum.
"O ko mākou one hānau kēia."	This is our birthplace/homeland (a Hawaiian phrase).
O.P.	O'ahu Prison, Hawai'i.
pa	Maori fortified village.
pa'ata	the Cook Island Maori word for the platform on which corpses were left to decay (in pre-Christian times).
pae'āina	a Hawaiian word meaning archipelago.
pahu	in Hawaiian, a drum made of sharkskin and used as an accompaniment to the hula.
pai	good (Hawai'i).
paiere	outrigger canoe, in the Ma'uke dialect of Cook Island Maori.
pākehā	Maori word for New Zealander of European ancestry.
palagi/palangi	a Samoan word for a white and western person, a person of European descent.
palaoa	the Hawaiian word for the sperm whale.
palapalai	different types of Hawaiian native fern, ranging in height from one to four feet.
palaoa	a Hawaiian term for the highly prized whale tooth pendant worn by those of chiefly rank.
pali	cliffs, in Hawaiian.
palolo	in Samoan, the name for coral worms that migrate once each year and are eaten as a delicacy.
pandanus	a tree whose leaves are soaked in the sea and dried in the sun for mats, baskets, etc.
papa	Hawaiian for flat surface, plain, reef, layer.
Papaā	a Cook Islands word used to denote a foreigner or European or white man. The word itself means four layers, and was given to Europeans when first seen because of their

	"wearing four layers of clothing", as seen by the natives.
pareu	female garment worn round the waist.
patu	to beat (eg. patu'd flax means beaten flax).
paua	New Zealand shellfish.
P.E.P.	a New Zealand government Primary Employment Programme, now-defunct.
pese Samoa	Samoan song.
P.I.C.	Pacific Islands Presbyterian Church.
pīkake	the Arabian jasmine, introduced to Hawai'i from India; very fragrant small white flowers often used for lei and other decorations.
pipi	New Zealand shellfish.
pisupo	Samoan for canned corned beef.
pito	New Zealand Maori for navel.
pohutukawa	a New Zealand native tree (*Metrosideros excelsa*), which is found all over the country, although its natural growing range is north of a line stretching from New Plymouth to Gisborne; it produces its red flowers at Christmas and is commonly known as the New Zealand Christmas tree.
porangi	New Zealand Maori for mad.
povi masima	Samoan for salted bully beef.
powhiri	in New Zealand Maori, the process by which people are welcomed on to a marae, or any other place in which these rituals are observed. The rituals are to ensure that the sanctity and dignity of everyone present is acknowledged, enhanced and/or restored.
pua	the Samoan word for the plumeria.
puha	New Zealand plant, the sour/sow thistle, rich in iron and Vitamin C.
pū'ili	in Hawaiian, bamboo rattles used for dancing.
puka	Hawaiian for anus.
puka papa'anga	in Cook Island Maori, a genealogical book.
pukeko	a multi-coloured New Zealand swamp hen.
punga/ponga	a tall New Zealand tree fern.
pupu	small New Zealand mollusc.
puriri	New Zealand native tree.
purua	a double canoe.
putatara	a traditional Maori trumpet, usually a conch shell.
pūtōrino	Maori musical wind instrument.
putuputuanga	Cook Islands phrase which means a gathering, assembling or mustering of people, particularly of women.
rangatahi	Maori for young people.
rangatira	Maori for chiefly class.
rangatiratanga	a New Zealand Maori term, from the root words rangatira, generally translated as "chief" or "leader" and tanga, commonly translated as "things" or "things to do with", so most often translated as chieftainship or leadership.
red rag	gang emblem.
reggo	car registration
reo	New Zealand Maori word for language.
sā	Samoan canoe, vessel; collective name of extended kin-group, e.g. Sā Nafanuā, the kin-group of Nafanuā, here used to connote an extended family group as passengers and crew on an early voyage of settlement.
saka	Samoan boiled bananas or breadfruit or taro.
scratch	Hawaiian slang for money.
siale tafa	an uncommon shrub or small tree (*Bhikkia terrandra*) which grows on coastal limestone cliffs in Tonga, the flowers of which are used in garlands.
sulu	Fijian for loincloth.
tagata	Samoan for human being.
taiaha	fighting weapon (Maori).
tangatawhenua	Maori for inhabitants, people of the land.
tangi	cry, weep, mourn, funeral.

taniwha	water guardian (Maori).
tapa	beaten bark cloth.
taro	a starchy tuber that is the staple of the diet of many Polynesian people; metaphorically the taro is the parent of the Hawaiian people.
tauihu	carved frontpiece of canoe (Maori)
taulaaitu	a Samoan word meaning priests.
taupata	Maori word for shrub.
tawatawa	a Cook Island word for mackerel.
te ao	New Zealand Maori for day, dawn, earth, or world.
te hau	the wind, in New Zealand Maori.
te hura	the hula.
te rangi	the heavens (Maori).
te reo	Maori language.
te tonuitanga	a New Zealand Maori phrase meaning "the time of the great gatherings when life was full" (an illusion from the well known lyric "E Pa to Hau", as discussed by Trixie Menzies in "Appreciation of a Poem", *Landfall* 167).
teatree	see manuka.
tekoteko	a New Zealand Maori word for the whakairo or carving at the head of a whare nui or meeting house, depicting the eponymous ancestor of the people to whom the house belongs.
tena koe	formal greeting to one person (in New Zealand Maori).
tena koe e koro	formal greeting to a male elder (in New Zealand Maori).
teuteu	To clean up (Samoan).
tihei mauri ora	a New Zealand Maori phrase meaning "I sneeze, it is life!".
ti-kouka	cabbage tree (Maori).
tinā	Samoan for mother.
tipi	to cut (Samoan)
tipuna	Maori for ancestors, male and female.
titoki	the New Zealand Maori word for a native tree, which produces oil.
tīvaevae	patchwork, work formed of patches or pieces sewn together; in particular a name given to the elaborate and brightly coloured appliqué bed quilts made by Cook Islands women.
toetoe	tall grass with spear-like flowers (Maori).
tohi	a New Zealand Maori ceremony before battle, to invoke the power and protection of the war god, Tumatauenga.
tohunga	priestly class (Maori).
tū kākāriki	a New Zealand Maori phrase meaning standing tall and green.
tuatua	a variety of New Zealand shellfish.
tuatua Maori	a Cook Island Maori phrase meaning speak Maori.
tuitui	a Cook Island Maori term for thread.
tukutuku	New Zealand Maori term for the woven panels on the walls of meeting houses.
tupuna	ancestors, in both New Zealand Maori and Cook Island Maori.
tupuna wahine	Maori for female ancestor.
turou	in Cook Island Maori, a song or chant of welcome or thanksgiving.
tūtū	Hawaiian for grandmother, grandaunt.
uenuku	Maori for rainbow.
uga	Nuiean for coconut crab.
'uhane	the Hawaiian word for soul, spirit, ghost.
'ulī'ulī	in Hawaiian a gourd rattle, containing seeds, with coloured feathers at the top, used for hula 'ulī'ulī.
'ulu	Hawaiian word for breadfruit.
ulu	Hawaiian word for grove.
umu	a Polynesian oven constructed with red hot stones and embers, specifically for cooking food.
uruātete	Cook Island Maori for seaside cliffs.

urupa	a New Zealand Maori word for burial grounds.
vunga	a tree (*Metrosideros collina*) which grows naturally at higher elevations, the red flowers of which are used in garlands and feature in songs and legends; currently common in the interior of Fiji but an introduction to Tonga from Fiji (possibly now extinct); known as rata in the Cook Islands, and ohi'a lehua in Hawaiian.
wa'a	canoe.
wāhine u'i	a Hawaiian phrase meaning beautiful woman.
wahine	women.
wai	the Hawaiian word for water.
waiata	song; to sing (Maori).
waka	in Maori, the word for vessel; often used to refer to one of the great ocean-going vessels that brought the ancestors of the Maori people from islands in the Pacific to New Zealand.
whaikorero	New Zealand Maori for speechmaking, especially fine and important oratory.
whakapapa	genealogy.
whana tukutahi	New Zealand Maori phrase for the all-out charge of a war party, precursor of the bayonet attack.
whanau	the New Zealand Maori word for family.
whare	New Zealand Maori for house, meeting house.
whare nui	a New Zealand Maori phrase meaning meeting house.
whare whakairo	Maori for a carved meeting house.
whenua	Maori for the land.

Index of titles

Index of poets by country